The SHORELINE CHEF

Creative Cuisine for Hawaiian Reef Fish

The SHORELINE CHEF
Creative Cuisine for Hawaiian Reef Fish

Elmer Guzman

WATERMARK
PUBLISHING

For my wonderful wife, Samantha — always there by my side —
and my beautiful daughters, Tatiana and Tatum,
who brighten all my days

ISBN 0-9720932-8-1

Library of Congress Control Number: 2003109409

Design by Leo Gonzalez

Production by Wendy Wakabayashi

Cover, pages 7, 14 – 16 photography by Lew Harrington
All other photography by Elmer and Samantha Guzman

Watermark Publishing
1000 Bishop Street, Suite 806
Honolulu, HI 96813
Telephone: Toll-free 1-866-900-BOOK
Web site: www.bookshawaii.net
e-mail: sales@bookshawaii.net

Printed in the Republic of Korea

CONTENTS

ACKNOWLEDGMENTS

Many thanks to Chef Sam Choy and James Lee for giving me the opportunity and the support to make my first cookbook a dream come true. Thank you to the kitchen staff at Sam Choy's Diamond Head Restaurant, headed by my right-hand man Aaron "Iron Chef" Fukuda, and including Fe Calaro, Dale Segawa, Eli Low, Ed Kahikolo, David Padua, Alika "Chew" Chung, Vishnu Om, Donovan Baro, Noel Gomes and Montrice Shumpert. Thank you also to the front-of-the-house wait staff and to my partner in crime, Dean Fujimoto.

My wonderful fish purveyors, Charlene and Chad from Ishimoto Fish Market in Chinatown, provide me with a great mixed bag for my fish menus. Ham Produce & Seafood also donates fresh island reef fish, while Uncle Hari Kojima always gives me additional knowledge and lots of great stories. Thank you to Alan Suzuki of Robert Mondavi for his wonderful wine and fish pairings and to Paul Ah Cook and Grant Sims for just knowing how to make it happen.

Special thanks to my Mom and Dad, Ernest and Jacinta Guzman, for raising me to be the man I am today, and to my father-in-law, Russell Jones, and Sandy Pieters, for babysitting my two crazy girls. To Randy Izuo for his words of wisdom, to Randy Francisco, who made organizing this book look so easy, and to Candice Lee, always a great supporter. Thank you to Betty Shimabukuro for all her help with my recipes and to Leo Gonzalez for his beautiful book design. And finally to George Engebretson, Duane Kurisu and Donovan Dela Cruz of Watermark Publishing, for believing in this project.

by Emeril Lagasse

Aloha!

In my many, many years of traveling to Hawai'i, my love for that special place has grown — and not just because of the food! This tropical paradise is truly a healing place: the beautiful ocean, lush landscape, gentle breezes, fragrant flowers and, especially, the island people and their warm aloha spirit.

I've spent a great deal of time in this dreamlike and enchanting environment, and each and every meal I've had has been exceptional. The food in Hawai'i is magical — from fish fries to lunchwagon fare to the incredible meals served in the hotels and restaurants. Hawai'i's cuisine makes the most of all the fresh local ingredients, including the many varieties of fish found in the blue Pacific. There is simply nothing better.

Having had the pleasure of hanging with my dear friend Chef Sam Choy, his beautiful family and his incredible staff, I have sampled and experienced wonderful Hawaiian reef fish prepared in any number of ways — in restaurants, at private homes and on the dock with local fishermen.

When I heard that my friend Chef Elmer Guzman was writing a book on island fish, I couldn't wait to get it in my hands. I consider him one of Hawai'i's great chefs, and I'm delighted that he's sharing his passion for creative cooking with the rest of us. This book is a long-awaited guide to Hawaiian reef and shoreline fish; I highly recommend it to anyone who enjoys cooking and eating fresh seafood. Mainland readers, by the way, might worry about finding some of the varieties included here. But rest assured: Elmer offers plenty of good tips on substitutions, too.

Enjoying reef and shoreline fish has always been part of the Hawaiian tradition. In *The Shoreline Chef*, you get not only the fascinating history of this tradition, but also a great guide on how to prepare these exotic fish. This book really does embody the spirit of the Islands. To Elmer I say, "Right on!" and to you I say, "Read on!" for a great aloha experience.

INTRODUCTION

Hawai'i people are spoiled. Here in the Islands, we can enjoy some of the world's best-eating fish on a daily basis — fish that other people have never even heard of. This was brought home to me when I developed a tasting menu of Hawaiian reef and shoreline fish for Sam Choy's Diamond Head, the restaurant where I work as executive chef. Mainland visitors began to tell me that — while they knew about ahi and mahimahi — they were unfamiliar with our tasty, plentiful reef fish — uhu, akule, kūmū and all the others.

When I was growing up on the Island of Maui, our Catholic Filipino family ate a lot of fish. Like many other families, we would fill our freezer with a mixed bag of reef fish caught by the local fishermen. And like most of those families, we would pull fish from the freezer and simply pan-fry them.

All of this got me to thinking: While local people catch or buy these fish on a regular basis, where do they go for more information on the various species, especially for recipes and preparation techniques? And where can visitors find a good fish cookbook or guidebook — a way to take these special Island flavors home with them? When I couldn't find any single comprehensive reference on the subject, I was inspired to create *The Shoreline Chef.*

This book is designed to help both home cooks and professionals become more familiar with Hawai'i's true island fishes. In my research, I found myself reading, interviewing and poking through lots of picturesque local fishmarkets. There were long days in Honolulu's Chinatown — smelling fresh fish, feeling their flesh, hunting for bargains. I made friends with the Ishimoto family and other knowledgeable fishmongers, talked story with little Chinese ladies about how they cooked what they bought, and pestered local fishing expert Hari Kojima daily about how to choose and cut fish.

In creating my menus and writing this book, I've tasted more than two dozen Hawaiian reef fish in a number of different preparations. It's a process I love, since each fish has its own distinctive characteristics: delicate kūmū, fishy-tasting kala, versatile moi, mū that resembles mahimahi in taste and texture, and 'ō'io that's so often used in fishcake.

One of the best things about life in Hawai'i is the culinary contributions of the diverse immigrant groups that comprise our population. Many of the unique traditions, techniques and ingredients brought by these groups have been adopted by the community as an integral part of our lifestyle. This book is no exception: It includes simple but delicious ethnic specialties that make these dishes easy on the palate and fun to shop for at our local and Asian grocery stores.

Availability of reef and shoreline fish is always a factor, of course, due to seasonality, rough weather and other conditions. And if you're trying these recipes anywhere but Hawai'i, chances are you won't find these fish anywhere. As a result, I've listed suggestions for substitutions on page 3.

I hope you enjoy the dishes you'll find here — cooking them, eating them, sharing them with family and friends. But before we tie on our aprons, following are a few things to consider when buying and preparing Hawaiian shoreline fish.

Buying the Best

When selecting fresh fish for your dinner table, it always helps to consult with a reputable fishmonger. He or she can tell you about the best buys of the day, offer tips on how to cook a certain type of fish, and tell you where the fish was caught, among other information. Here are a few pointers that will help you select the best fish and maximize your dining experience. They'll help you save worry, time and money.

- Fresh fish won't smell fishy!!
- Eyes should appear full and clear, not cloudy and sunken.
- Check the gills for a bright red color that is not slimy and discolored.
- Ask if you can touch the fish. It should feel firm, not soft, and the fingertips shouldn't leave any indentation.
- Make sure they clean the fish for you (or clean it yourself). The guts of a dead fish will taint the flesh around it.
- Scales should be intact and adhere tightly to the skin.
- Beware of fish that is unusually cheap; it's probably been kept in cold storage and is far from fresh.

Storing Your Fish

After purchasing fresh fish either whole or filleted, be sure to chill it immediately or it will start losing its freshness. Fish should be wrapped in clear wrap and placed in the refrigerator no more than a day or two after purchase. Make sure the temperature of the refrigerator is between 32° and 38° F. Pack the fish in ice or in a damp towel that will hold in moisture and keep it from drying out, thereby reducing weight loss. If the fish are whole, store them on their stomachs parallel to each other, to prevent them from being crushed. And finally, if you purchase a fish that is bent, usually from bad handling or rigor mortis, don't try to straighten it out, as you'll likely damage the flesh.

A Word About Ciguatera

Ciguatera fish poisoning is endemic wherever coral fish are a food source. You can catch ciguatera by eating reef fish tainted with ciguatoxins, which colonize in coral beds. The toxins first affect the small, coral-grazing fish and are then passed up the food chain to you and me. It isn't uncommon for a fish on one side of the island to be poisonous while the same species on the other side is safe to eat. If you're not sure about purchasing island reef fish, patronize a reputable fishmarket licensed to sell fish. For you fishermen, the Cigua-Check Test™ Fish Poison Kit is commercially available at your local fishing supplies store.

FISH SUBSTITUTIONS

Barracuda	Rainbow Runner
Bonefish	Milkfish
Emperor	Mahimahi, Halibut, Monchong
Flagtail	Perch
Goatfish	Red Mullet, Smelt
Grouper	Swordfish, Opah
Jack/Trevally	Pompano, Shark, Swordfish
Mullet	Frozen Mullet available year-round, Catfish
Scad	Mackerel, Saba
Scorpionfish	Rockfish, Monkfish, Cod
Snapper	Redfish, 'Ōpakapaka, Onaga; all types of Snapper
Surgeonfish	
Threadfin	Rainbow Trout, Salmon, Flounder, Hamachi, Marlin, Escolar
Wrasse	

Fish	Flavor	Texture	Cooking Methods	Availability
Barracuda				
Kākū (Great Barracuda)	R	M	G/SM/ST	A
Bonefish				
'Ō'io (Small Mouth Bonefish)	MOD	T	R/ST	A
Emperor				
Mū (Big Eye Emperor)	D	M	RO/ST	A
Flagtail				
Āholehole (Hawaiian Flagtail)	D	T	SA	W
Goatfish (Weke)				
Kūmū (White Saddle Goatfish)	D	T	ST/SA/G	A
Weke'ā (Yellowstriped Goatfish)	MOD	T	ST/SA/G/P	A
Moano (Many Bar Goatfish)	MOD	T	SA/G	A
'Oama (Juvenile Goatfish)	MOD	T	SA	S
Grouper				
Hāpu'upu'u (Hawaiian Seabass)	MOD	M	SA/P/ST	A
Roi (Peacock Grouper)	D	M	ST/P/SA	A
Jack/Trevally (Ulua)				
Butaguchi (Thicklipped Jack)	D	M	GR/P/R/RO	A
'Omilu (Blue Fin Trevally)	MOD	M	G/P/R/RO/ST	A
Papio (Juvenile Jack)	D	M	G/P/R/RO	A

Fish	Flavor	Texture	Cooking Methods	Availability
Mullet 'Ama'ama (Striped Mullet)	MOD	M	P/ST/RO	SP/S/F
Parrotfish (Uhu) Uhu uli'uli (Speckled Parrotfish)	MOD	F	P/ST	A
Scad 'Ōpelu (Mackerel Scad)	R	T	R/SA	A
Akule (Big Eye Scad)	R	T	R/SA	A
Scorpionfish Nohu (Titan Scorpionfish)	D	F	P/SA/ST	A
Snapper Toau (Blacktail Snapper)	MOD	M	SA/ST	A
Taape (Bluestripe Snapper)	MOD	M	SA/ST	A
Surgeonfish Manini (Convict Surgeonfish)	R	M	G/P/SA	A
Kala (Bluespine Unicornfish)	R	F	G/R	A
Threadfin Moi (Six Fingered Threadfin)	D	T	ALL	A
Wrasse 'A'awa (Hawaiian Hogfish)	R	T	SA	A
Nabeta (Peacock Wrasse)	D	T	SA	W/S

Flavor: **D**–Delicate, **Mod**–Moderate, **R**–Robust

Texture: **F**–Firm, **M**–Medium, **T**–Tender

Cooking Method: **G**–Grilled, **P**–Poached, **R**–Raw, **RO**–Roasted, **SA**–Sautéed, **S**–Seared, **SM**–Smoked, **ST**–Steamed

Availability: **W**–Winter, **SP**–Spring, **S**–Summer, **F**–Fall, **A**–All Seasons

WINE AND FISH MATRIX

FISH	WINES				RED
	DRY ──────────────➤ SEMI-SWEET				
	PINOT GRIGIO	FUMÉ BLANC	CHARDONNAY	J. RIESLING	PINOT NOIR
Barracuda		•		•	
Bonefish	•			•	
Emperor	•		•		
Flagtail	•			•	
Goatfish		•		•	
Grouper	•		•		
Jack/Trevally	•		•		
Mullet	•			•	
Parrotfish		•	•		
Scad		•			•
Scorpionfish	•			•	
Snapper	•			•	
Surgeonfish		•		•	
Threadfin	•			•	
Wrasse		•	•		

Courtesy Robert Mondavi Winery

Top: Charbroiled Whole
Moano. Right: Poached
Mullet in Chiso Fennel
Broth.

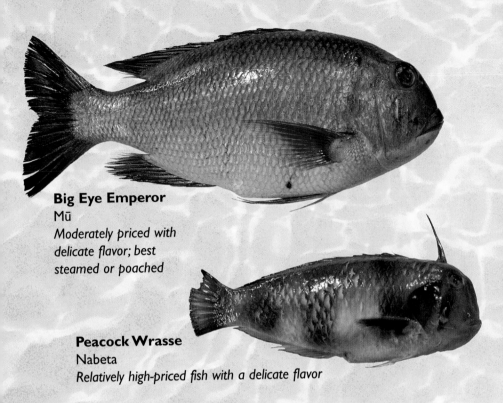

Big Eye Emperor
Mū
Moderately priced with
delicate flavor; best
steamed or poached

Peacock Wrasse
Nabeta
Relatively high-priced fish with a delicate flavor

Hawaiian Hogfish
A'awa
Member of the wrasse
family; tasty reef fish that
comes in vibrant colors

Six Fingered
Threadfin
Moi
Versatile bottom feeder once reserved for royalty;
holds up well under any cooking method

Big Eye Scad
Akule
*Silvery blue-green
fish; excellent
when prepared
as poke*

Mackerel Scad
Ōpelu
*Silvery blue-green fish; readily available at fishmarkets,
grocery stores and roadside stands*

Striped Mullet
'Ama'ama
*Long-bodied fish with large scales; bottom
feeder that thrives in brackish water*

Speckled Parrotfish
Uhu Uli'uli
*One of the main producers of sand;
moderate flavor and tender texture,
great for steaming*

White Saddle Goatfish
Kūmū
Relatively pricey bottom feeder with delicate flavor

Red Goatfish
Weke 'Ula
Bottom feeder with moderate flavor; less expensive than certain other goatfish

Many Bar Goatfish
Moano
Bottom feeder; one of the tastiest of reef fish, selling at higher prices than most

Juvenile Goatfish
'Oama
Weke under seven inches in length that doesn't require cleaning; illegal to sell

Great Barracuda
Kākū
Predator fish usually found alone or in small schools; robust flesh of medium texture

Hawaiian Seabass
Hāpuʻupuʻu
Grouper with flavor ranging from delicate to moderate

Peacock Grouper
Roi
Medium textured flesh ideal for use in chowders, jambalaya and stews

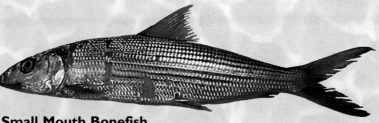

Small Mouth Bonefish
ʻŌʻio
Bottom feeder with many tiny bones; most commonly used in fishcake

Titan Scorpionfish
Nohu
Popular, moderately priced predator fish; great in soups, broths and bouillabaisse

Flagtail
Āholehole
Silvery fish with a delicate flavor and tender texture; swims in dense schools close to the reef

Bluefin Trevally
Ōmilu
Tasty fish with firm flesh; smaller member of the ulua (jack/trevally) family

Giant Trevally
White Ulua
Gamefish and member of the jack/trevally family; medium to firm meat with moderate taste

Bluestripe Snapper
Taape
Very inexpensive reef fish introduced from the Marquesas in 1958

Blacktail Snapper
Toau
Inexpensive fish ideal for sautéeing or deep frying; introduced from Moorea in 1956

Bluespine Unicornfish
Kala
Member of the surgeonfish family; a hearty fish with a seaweed flavor

Convict Tang
Manini
Member of the surgeonfish family named for its vertical stripes; robust flavor at bargain prices

Top: Pan Fried To'au with Fried Garlic Edamame Sauce and Pea Shoot Salad. Left: Filipino-Influenced Moi Ceviche.

FISH CUTTING GUIDE

by Hari Kojima

Hi, gang! Hari here!

Although there are many ways to fillet a fish, I find that the simplest way to get fillets is to buy them in that form! Nah, nah, nah! Only kidding!

Here's how to fillet fish for real: Always begin by scaling the fish. It makes for much easier cutting with the scales removed.

1. Clean the fish, including removal of the gills and the innards. Then rinse thoroughly.

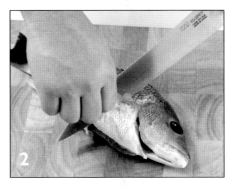

2. You can take off the head by cutting just to the rear of the pectoral fins, one side at a time.

3. Then cut down to the bone and right through it. (Bigger fish might require the use of a rubber mallet.)

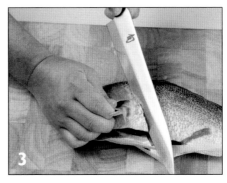

4. Now that the fish is headless, you can begin the process of filleting. With the fish on its side, place your knife on the top of the dorsal fin and cut as close to the center bone as possible.

5. Then continue at the bottom of the fish and cut to the center bone again. Now the only area where the fish is connected is at the center part of the center bone.

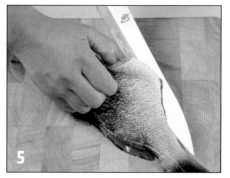

6. From the tail area, lift the fillet and gently cut toward the front of the fish. Now you've got one fillet off.

7. Continue by turning the fish over and repeating the process. No sweat ! And don't forget: The heads — especially of the Hawaiian snappers — make excellent soups. (But, of course, that's a whole other book.)

Enjoy!

BARRACUDA

Kākū

Many people in Hawai'i are afraid of eating barracuda, better known locally as kākū, because of its appearance. With its elongated body and sharp teeth, the Great Barracuda looks just plain mean. Kākū is a predator of the sea, feeding mostly on other small fish. Usually, you'll find it alone or in small groups, often in shallow waters close to shore. A kākū can grow up to six feet long and weigh about 100 pounds. The ones usually available in fish stores are two- to three-pounders, just right for a family dinner.

Charlene, a friend of mine at Ishimoto Fish Market in Chinatown, suggested that I try this fish steamed Chinese-style. I haven't been afraid of a barracuda since!

Kākū is robust, with medium texture, and best cooked using a moist heating method, such as poaching, steaming and, believe it or not, smoking. Following are a few dishes to whet your appetite.

PROSCIUTTO-WRAPPED KĀKŪ WITH A CREAMY PEA RISOTTO

This dish is a play on the traditional Filipino pork-and-peas dish called Pork Quesatis, using prosciutto (Italian cured pork) and a creamy pea risotto.

2	4- to 6-oz. kākū fillets (from 3- to 4-lb. whole fish)
6 sheets	prosciutto
2 tbsp.	salad oil
	fresh cracked black pepper to taste

Season kākū fillet with fresh cracked black pepper. Wrap each piece of kākū in a prosciutto sheet. In a sauté pan, heat oil. Sear kākū 2-3 minutes on each side. Serve over Creamy Pea Risotto.

Creamy Pea Risotto

4 oz.	butter
4 tbsp.	diced onions
I tsp.	minced garlic
2 cups	arborio rice
5-3/4 cups	clam juice
2 tbsp.	Parmesan cheese
I cup	frozen peas

Heat 3 oz. butter in a sauté pan. Add onions and garlic; sauté 2 minutes. Do not allow to brown. Add rice and stir to coat with butter. Slowly add clam juice and continue to stir until clam juice evaporates, 15-20 minutes. Add Parmesan cheese, remaining I oz. butter and peas, then season. Serves 4-6.

Recommended wine: Johannisberg Riesling

SMOKED KĀKŪ SALAD WITH ISLAND MANGO DRESSING

This colorful and tasty dish combines kiawe-smoked kākū with a mouth-watering salad.

Smoked Kākū

4 to 6	3-oz. kākū fillets (from 2-1/2- to 3-lb. whole kākū)
1 tbsp. 2 tsp.	kosher salt
2 tbsp.	granulated sugar
1-1/2 cups	damp mango or kiawe chips

Combine salt and sugar. Lightly sprinkle mixture on surface of fillet and let sit for 30-45 minutes. Place mango or kiawe chips in a 12-in. wok. Heat wok until chips start smoldering. Place well-oiled 8-in. rack in the wok, 3 in. above chips. The chips should begin smoking in 10-15 minutes. Place fish on oiled rack, cover wok with a sheet of foil to make sure the smoke doesn't escape. Smoke for 10 minutes or until done.

Island Mango Dressing

2 cups	mango puree
1 tsp.	minced garlic
1 cup	white vinegar
3 tbsp.	granulated sugar
1 tbsp.	minced cilantro
1 tsp.	fresh cracked black pepper
3 cups	salad oil
1-1/4 cups	ripe diced island mango
	salt and pepper to taste

Combine mango puree, garlic, vinegar, sugar, cilantro and fresh cracked pepper. Stir well. Slowly whisk in oil until all ingredients are mixed. Season with salt and pepper and fold in diced mango.

Smoked Kākū Salad

1	avocado, sliced (optional)
6 sheets	deep-fried wonton squares
8 cups	mixed greens
3 tbsp.	red onions, thinly sliced
	Smoked Kākū
1/4 cup	Island Mango Dressing

Divide avocado among 4 plates. Top with crispy wonton, followed by the greens and onions. Add fish, then drizzle with dressing. Serves 4.

Recommended wine: Johannisberg Riesling

POACHED KĀKŪ ON NALO GREENS WITH WARM HAUʻULA TOMATO VINAIGRETTE

The poached kākū is accentuated with a broth composed of ginger, lemongrass and kaffir lime. This combination gives it a rich flavor.

4	3- to 4-oz. kākū fillets (from 1-1/4- to 1-1/2-lb. whole kākū, cleaned and scaled)
1 qt.	Basic Fish Stock (see Basic Recipes; may substitute clam juice or chicken stock)
1 in.	ginger, smashed
1	bay leaf
1 tsp.	whole black peppercorn
1 stalk	lemongrass, smashed (optional)
2	kaffir lime leaves (optional)
1/2	lemon
1 lb.	Nalo greens
	salt and pepper to taste

In a pot combine fish stock, ginger, bay leaf, peppercorns, lemongrass and kaffir leaf. Squeeze juice from lemon half into pot; add lemon skin as well. Simmer for 20-30 minutes and strain. Transfer seasoned stock to a saucepan over medium/low heat. Place fillets in liquid and poach 5-8 minutes. Remove fish with a slotted spatula and gently place on the Nalo greens. Drizzle fish with Warm Hauʻula Tomato Vinaigrette.

Warm Hauʻula Tomato Vinaigrette

1 cup	extra virgin olive oil
1/4 cup	apple cider vinegar
1 tsp.	minced ginger
1 tsp.	minced garlic
1 tbsp.	julienned basil
4	minced anchovy fillets (optional)
2 tsp.	capers
1 tbsp.	granulated sugar
	juice of 1/2 lemon
1 cup	diced Hauʻula tomatoes
	salt and pepper to taste

Combine all ingredients except tomatoes, salt and pepper in a saucepan and heat to a simmer. Fold in the tomato and season with salt and pepper. Serves 4-6.

Recommended wine: Fumé Blanc

4	whole kākū (1-1/4 to 1-1/2 lbs.), cleaned and scaled
	salt and pepper to taste
	sesame oil for stir-frying
1 lb.	snow peas

Season fish with salt and pepper. Steam for 10-12 minutes in a store-bought steamer. Heat sesame oil in a sauté pan. Add snow peas and sauté 3 minutes or until tender. Add 2 tbsp. water to keep snow peas from scorching. Allow heat and water to create steam. Season. Arrange peas on platter, place whole kākū in center and top with a generous serving of black bean sauce. Garnish with fresh cilantro sprigs. Serves 4-6.

Fermented Black Bean Sauce

2 tbsp.	sesame oil
1 tbsp.	minced ginger
1 tbsp.	minced garlic
1 cup	fermented black beans, rinsed and chopped
1 cup	diced yellow onions
1/2 cup	diced celery
1 cup	chicken broth
1/2 cup	shoyu
1/2 cup	oyster sauce
1 cup	water
1/2 cup	diced red bell pepper
4 tbsp.	sliced green onion
3 tbsp.	cornstarch dissolved in 1/4 cup water
6 tbsp.	sugar

Heat sesame oil in a sauce pan. Add ginger, garlic and black beans; sauté 2 minutes. Add onions and celery; sauté 2 minutes. Deglaze pan with chicken broth. Add shoyu, oyster sauce and water. Bring to a boil. Add red bell pepper and green onions. Thicken with cornstarch slurry and fold in sugar.

Recommended wines: Fumé Blanc, Sauvignon Blanc

BONEFISH

BONEFISH

ʻŌʻio

Bonefish, known by its Hawaiian name, ʻōʻio, is commonly found in shallow sandy bottoms, feeding on worms, crustaceans or any small organisms living beneath the sand. Bonefish, which have many tiny bones in their flesh, are often found in fish markets as what appears to be ground-up fish in a stainless steel bowl on ice. The scraping of a butter-flied bonefish, or the pressing of the whole fish, gives it the appearance of ground meat for fish cake — which is what this fish is most famous for. It's often said that you should keep bonefish refrigerated for a week or so, in order to allow the fish to start breaking down. While this may be true, who has the time? Go ahead and butterfly the bonefish and start scraping as soon as you buy it. Or just buy it already prepared and refrigerate that.

Here are a few recipes that you can enjoy immediately, including Lomi Lomi ʻŌʻio, which can be eaten raw and served as a pūpū. This recipe was inspired by Judy Choy, our hostess at Sam Choy's Diamond Head restaurant, who shared with me an ʻōʻio patty recipe from her childhood days.

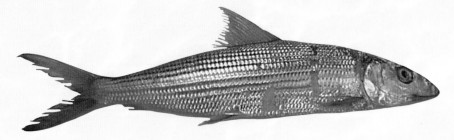

'ŌʻIO GYOZA
WITH WASABI SOY LIME DIPPING SAUCE

This seafood version of gyoza (a Japanese-style potsticker) can complement nearly any meal or gathering.

'Ōʻio Gyoza Filling

10 oz.	ground ʻōʻio (from 2-lb. whole fish)
1/2 tsp.	minced garlic
1	egg
1 tbsp.	sliced green onion
2 tsp.	ground black pepper
1-1/2 tbsp.	oyster sauce
1 tsp.	soy sauce
1 tsp.	sesame oil
1 tsp.	garlic chili paste
1/4 cup	chopped water chestnuts
30	won ton pi wrappers

Combine all ingredients except the won ton pi and chill. To prepare gyoza, place won ton pi on work surface. Place 1/2-3/4 oz. of filling in the center of the won ton pi. Brush edges with water and fold to form a half-moon shape. In a non-stick pan, heat 2 tbsp. salad oil, and place gyoza in the pan to crisp the bottoms. Once gyoza is crispy, add 1/4 cup water to pan and cover. Cover and steam for 3-4 minutes; remove cover, allowing water to evaporate, then re-crisp gyoza an additional 1-2 minutes. Serve with dipping sauce. Makes 30 pieces; serves 4-6.

Wasabi Soy Lime Dipping Sauce

1/2 cup	granulated sugar
1/2 cup	soy sauce
1/4 cup	rice wine vinegar
3/4 cup	lime juice
1 tsp.	minced garlic
1/4 cup	ginger, smashed
2 tbsp.	wasabi paste

Combine, mix well and let sit for 30 minutes; strain. Yields 2-1/4 cups.

Recommended wine: Pinot Grigio

'Ō'IO PATTIES WITH MUSTARD SOY SAUCE

Here's a healthy fish alternative to the traditional hamburger. It is also useful as a meat substitute in sandwiches.

16 oz.	'ō'io meat (from 3-lb. whole fish)
3 oz.	diced char siu pork
2 tbsp.	sliced green onion
2 tbsp.	chopped water chestnuts
1	whole egg
	salt and pepper to taste
6 tbsp.	salad oil

Mix all ingredients except oil and divide portions into patties 1/2 in. thick and 2 in. across. Chill in a baking pan and set aside until ready to use. Heat oil over medium heat and sear patties 2-3 minutes on each side. Serve with mustard soy sauce. Serves 4-6.

Mustard Soy Sauce

1 tbsp.	soy sauce
1 tbsp.	dry mustard
1 cup	Basic Butter Sauce (see Basic Recipes)

Combine soy sauce and dry mustard, then fold into Basic Butter Sauce.

Recommended wine: Johannisberg Riesling

LOMI LOMI 'Ō'IO

Charlene at Ishimoto Fish Market introduced me to this wonderful fish dish. It is very simple and tastes great with poi. Awa (milkfish) can be used as a substitute.

8 oz.	'ō'io meat (from 1-1/2- to 2-lb. whole fish)
2 tbsp.	diced onion
1 tbsp.	sliced green onion
1 tbsp.	chopped thick ogo
1/2 tsp.	Hawaiian salt
1 tsp.	inamona
1 tsp.	chopped limu-kohu (seaweed)
1	minced Hawaiian chili pepper (optional)

Combine all ingredients. Chill at least 30 minutes. Serves 4-6.

Recommended wine: Johannisberg Riesling

EMPEROR

BIG-EYE EMPEROR

Mū

The big-eye emperor, better known in the Islands as mū, is best when prepared by moist heat cooking, such as steaming or poaching. Mū can usually be found in fishmarkets weighing from three to five pounds and ranging in price between $3.95 and $6 per pound, depending upon availability. It is a moderately priced and popular fish, which is why it usually sells out in the markets. Mū has a delicate flavor, with a medium texture to its flesh, similar to mahimahi. It uses its human-like molars to crush hard-shelled invertebrates, sea urchins and small fishes.

Included here are recipes to let you to taste its delicate flavor, such as Baked Miso Crab Glazed Mū, a version that's steamed with Asian confit and another that offers an alternative to cold ginger chicken.

COLD GINGER SCALLION MŪ

4-5	3 oz. mū fillet (from 3- to 4-lb. whole fish)
4 cups	chicken stock (may substitute clam juice or fish stock)
1 finger	ginger, smashed
1 tsp.	whole black pepper
1	whole head garlic cut in half
	salt to taste
	green onion stems (optional)

In a stock pot, combine all ingredients except the mū. Bring to a boil and simmer for 5 minutes. Season with salt and pepper. Place mū fillets in stock and poach for 6 to 8 minutes or until done. With a slotted spatula, slowly remove fish from stock; refrigerate.

Ginger Scallion Sauce

1/4 cup	minced ginger
1/4 cup	minced green onion
1 tsp.	soy sauce
1 tbsp.	sesame oil
1/2 cup	peanut oil
	salt and pepper to taste

Combine all ingredients. Spread over cooled, poached mū 5-10 minutes prior to serving. Serve mū on a bed of shredded head cabbage or mixed greens. Serves 4-6.

Recommended wines: Chardonnay, Pinot Grigio

BAKED MISO CRAB GLAZED MŪ

The miso and crab meat add flavor that perfectly complements the baked mū.

4-5	3-oz. mū fillet (from 3- to 4-lb. whole fish)
	salt and pepper to taste

Miso Crab Glaze

1	egg
1/4 tsp.	minced garlic
	juice of 1 lemon
1 tbsp.	granulated sugar
1 cup	salad oil
1 tbsp.	minced cilantro
	salt and pepper to taste
4 oz.	blue crab claw meat (may substitute pasteurized or imitation crab meat)

Preheat oven to 350 degrees. Whisk together egg, garlic, lemon juice and sugar in a stainless steel bowl. Slowly whisk in oil until dressing starts to thicken. Fold in cilantro and season with salt and pepper. Fold in crabmeat. Season mū fillets with salt and pepper; place on a well-oiled baking pan. Spoon miso glaze over fillets and bake 15-20 minutes. Serve on a bed of stir-fried baby bok choy. Serves 4-6.

Recommended wine: Chardonnay

BAKED ARTICHOKE WITH SPICY MŪ IMPERIAL

In New Orleans there are two ways of stuffing an artichoke: 1) the traditional style between the leaves or artichoke halves and 2) placing the stuffing in the cavity.

6	whole cleaned artichoke
5 sprigs	fresh thyme
1 tbsp.	whole black peppercorns
3	bay leaves
5	lemons, cut in half and squeezed
	salt to taste
	water to cover

To prepare artichokes, cut 1 in. from the top and 1 in. from the stem of each. Trim outer leaves at base of artichoke with a paring knife until you reach the yellowish-green heart. Rub all exposed areas of the artichoke with lemon half to prevent discoloration. Add spices and squeezed lemons to water and season with salt. Bring water to a boil. The acid from the lemons helps keep the color of the artichokes vibrant. Cook artichokes 45 minutes or until a knife goes in easily. Submerge in ice water to stop the cooking process.

Spicy Mū Imperial

1 lb.	diced mū
1 tbsp.	vegetable oil
3/4 cup	chopped onions
1/4 cup	chopped green bell peppers
1/4 cup	chopped celery
1 tbsp.	minced garlic
2 tbsp.	minced parsley
1 cup	mayonnaise
2 tbsp.	Dijon mustard
1/4 tsp.	Tabasco sauce
	salt and pepper to taste
1/4 cup	panko
6	whole artichokes cooked, cut in half, choke removed (see opposite page)
1 tsp.	Chef E Spice (see Basic Recipes)

Preheat oven to 400 degrees. Heat oil in a sauté pan over high heat. Add onion, bell pepper and celery. Sauté 5 minutes or until wilted. Add mū and cook about 5 minutes, stirring occasionally. Remove from heat and let cool about 30 minutes. In a mixing bowl combine mū mixture with garlic, parsley, 3/4 cup mayonnaise, mustard and Tabasco. Mix well. Add salt and pepper to adjust seasoning. Spoon mixture into artichoke halves. Combine panko, remaining mayonnaise and Chef E Spice. Spread over mū mixture and bake 20-30 minutes or until bubbly and brown. Serves 12.

Recommended wine: Pinot Grigio

STEAMED MŪ TOPPED WITH ASIAN ONION CONFIT AND WOK-FRIED DRIED EBI LONG BEANS

The addition of Chinese long beans and dried ebi (shrimp) provides this dish with crunch. While confit is a way of preserving an ingredient in its own fat, this dish uses vegetable oil instead.

4-5	3-oz. mū fillets (from 3- to 4-lb. whole fish)
	salt and pepper to taste

Season fillets with salt and pepper. Steam in a bamboo steamer 8-10 minutes.

Asian Onion Confit

1-1/2 cups	onion, thinly sliced
2 tbsp.	sliced green onion
1 tbsp.	fine julienned ginger
1/2 tbsp.	minced garlic
1 tbsp.	sesame oil
1/4 cup	chopped fresh cilantro
2 tbsp.	soy sauce
1/4 cup	julienned lup chong (sweet Chinese sausage, optional)
1 tbsp.	minced fermented Chinese black beans (optional)
1-1/4 cups	salad oil
	salt and pepper to taste

Combine all ingredients except oil in a stainless steel bowl and mix well. Heat oil in a wok over high heat until it begins to smoke. Pour heated oil over vegetables and stir well. Cool. Season with salt and pepper.

Wok-Fried Dried Ebi Long Beans

1/4 cup	salad oil
3 cups	Chinese long beans cut into 2-in. portions
3/4 cup	julienned red onion
2 tbsp.	dried ebi (shrimp)
2 tsp.	dashi
1 tsp.	garlic chili paste
	salt and pepper to taste

Heat oil in a wok until it begins to smoke. Sauté long beans until blistered. Add onions and dried ebi and sauté 2 minutes. Sprinkle with dashi and garlic chili paste and season with salt and pepper. Place wok-fried dried ebi long beans on the center of the plate. Gently place steamed mū on long beans and top with Asian Onion Confit. Serves 4-6.

Recommended wine: Pinot Grigio

FLAGTAIL

Āholehole

Flagtail, or āholehole, is an ordinary-looking, silvery fish that usually swims in a dense school and remains close to the reef for protection from larger fish. It often feeds at night on zooplankton. The flagtail has a delicate flavor and a tender texture; it is both affordable and good eating. People usually want to scale and gut this fish, but after it's filleted, it doesn't yield much meat. The best way to prepare it is to simply pan fry it until it's thoroughly cooked, then serve it with a sauce of shoyu and Hawaiian chili pepper water on the side.

Following are a few options to help you spice up your cooking repertoire. I've also included a smothered dish New Orleans-style, which I learned from Emeril Lagasse. Here, too, is a simple, oven-roasted dish that can help you feed an army without feeling overwhelmed.

ĀHOLEHOLE ETOUFFÉE

In New Orleans, etouffée means to cook something in its own juices or in water. This simple dish tastes great over steamed rice.

6	whole āholehole (4 oz. ea.)
3 oz.	butter
	salt and pepper to taste
2 cups	diced yellow onions
1 cup	diced celery
1 cup	diced green bell pepper
2 tsp.	minced garlic
2 tsp.	Chef E Spice (see Basic Recipes)
2 tbsp.	flour
3 cups	water
	splash of Tabasco
	splash Worcestershire sauce
1/2 cup	sliced green onions
1 tbsp.	chopped parsley

Melt butter in a large sauté pan over medium heat. Season āholehole with salt and pepper. Sear 2-3 minutes on each side until done; remove from pan. To the same pan add onions, celery and green bell peppers. Sauté about 5 minutes. Add garlic and cook 2 minutes. Add Chef E Spice. Dissolve flour in water and add to vegetable mixture. Simmer until mixture begins to thicken. Season with Tabasco and Worcestershire sauces. Garnish with green onions and chopped parsley. Spoon sauce over sautéed fish. Serve with steamed rice. Serves 4-6.

Recommended wines: Pinot Grigio, Chardonnay

OVEN-ROASTED ĀHOLEHOLE WITH ASIAN OIL

This fish tends to be more succulent and moist when cooked or roasted whole.

6	whole āholehole (5-6 oz. ea.), scaled and gutted
	salt and pepper to taste
1 cup	Asian Oil (see Basic Recipes)
3 tbsp.	soy sauce
	Basic Garlic Butter (see Basic Recipes)

Preheat oven to 425 degrees. Score āholehole skin, making X cuts. Season all over with salt and pepper. Rub Asian Oil into score marks and fish cavities. Place fish on a well-oiled sheet pan and drizzle with soy sauce. Roast 10-15 minutes. Top each fish with a dab of garlic butter for added flavor. Serves 4-6.

Recommended wine: Johannisberg Riesling

FURIKAKE-DUSTED ĀHOLEHOLE ON BROWN RICE SUSHI SALAD

6   whole āholehole (4-5 oz. ea.), scaled and gutted
3 tbsp.   furikake rice seasoning
            salad oil to sear

Season fish with furikake. Heat oil in a sauté pan and sear fish
3-4 minutes on each side.

Brown Sushi Rice

3 cups   short-grain brown rice
3-1/2 cups water
2 tbsp.   sake (optional)
4-in. piece konbu
1/3 cup   rice wine vinegar
3 tbsp.   mirin

Wash rice and drain. Place in pressure cooker with water, sake and
konbu and let sit for 3 hours. This will make the rice much more
tender and will infuse it with the flavors of the other ingredients.
Cook rice 20 minutes over low heat. (If using white rice, soak for
1 hour and use a rice cooker.) Remove from heat and let sit
15 minutes. Combine rice wine vinegar and mirin. Remove konbu
from rice and place in a large, flat container. Sprinkle with vinegar
mixture. Use a spatula to mix and turn the rice with a cutting
motion while fanning it vigorously until it shines.

Brown Rice Sushi Salad

4 cups	brown sushi rice
1/3 cup	reconstituted wakame
3 tbsp.	toasted white sesame seeds
1/3 cup	carrot, thinly sliced and blanched
2 tbsp.	white onion, thinly sliced
10 ea.	chiso leaves, thinly sliced for garnish
	pickled ginger, for garnish

Combine sushi rice with wakame, sesame seeds, carrots and onions. Garnish with chiso and serve with pickled ginger on the side. Top salad with furikake-dusted fish. Serves 4-6.

Recommended wine: Johannisberg Riesling

GOATFISH

RED WEKE
3.50 LB

GOATFISH

Kūmū • Moano • 'Oama • Weke 'Ula

Goatfish, or weke, are among the tastiest — and highest priced — of our island reef fish. They range from the expensive kūmū and moano to the more affordable weke'ā and red goatfish. The flavor also varies from delicate to moderate. They are easily recognized by their barbel, that distinctive little feature reminiscent of a goat's beard. Goatfish are bottom dwellers that feed on worms, crustaceans and invertebrates.

Weke under seven inches long are called 'oama. 'Oama are illegal to sell, so you'll have to go out and have fun catching them yourself. One thing I like about these little fish is that you don't have to clean them. Simply season and deep fry until extra crispy.

Because goatfish come in so many different varieties, this section includes a few extra dishes, including Banana Leaf Wrapped Moano, Charbroiled Whole Kūmū, and baked weke in a spicy peanut sauce, inspired by sous chef Aaron of Sam Choy's Diamond Head.

The garlic butter used to baste this grilled dish both seasons the fish and keeps it moist.

5-6	whole kūmū (12 oz. ea.)
1 cup	extra virgin olive oil
2 sprigs	fresh thyme
2 sprigs	fresh rosemary
3 cloves	garlic, smashed
1 tsp.	whole black peppercorns
1	bay leaf
	salt and fresh cracked pepper to taste
	Basic Herb Oil (see Basic Recipes)

Combine all ingredients except fish and let sit at least 24 hours.

Garlic Butter for Seafood

1 lb.	softened unsalted butter
1/4 cup	white wine (optional)
1/4 cup	minced garlic
	juice of 1 lemon
1 tsp.	minced parsley
	splash of Tabasco sauce
	splash of Worcestershire sauce

Combine well. Season fish with salt and fresh cracked pepper. Marinate in Basic Herb Oil 1 hour. Grill fish over medium heat, basting periodically with garlic butter, for 20-30 minutes. Serves 4-6.

Recommended wines: Fumé Blanc, Chardonnay

STEAMED AROMATIC KŪMŪ

Kūmū is a very delicate fish. The natural ingredients in this recipe bring out a wonderful medley of flavors.

6	3- to 4-oz. kūmū fillets (from 3 whole kūmū, 1-1/4 lbs. ea.)
3 cups	quartered shiitake mushroom
3 cups	choi sum, in 1-in. pieces
2 tbsp.	orange juice
2 tbsp.	lemon juice
	zest of 2 oranges
6	Hawaiian chili peppers (or 1/4 oz. chili pepper flakes)
1	lemongrass stalk, sliced
5-6	kaffir lime leaves (may substitute herbs such as tarragon, thyme or dill)
	salt and pepper to taste

Place mushrooms and choi sum in the bottom of a bowl. Lay kūmū fillets on top of vegetables. Pour orange juice and lemon juice over fish. Sprinkle each fillet with orange zest, two slices of lemongrass, a kaffir lime leaf, chili peppers, salt and pepper. Seal bowl with plastic wrap. Place in a steamer basket over boiling water and steam for 25 minutes. Serves 4-6.

Recommended wine: Johannisberg Riesling

BAKED WHOLE KŪMŪ IN SALT CRUST

This dish incorporates a French technique in which the whole fish steams in a salt and flour crust, keeping it moist and flavorful.

3	whole kūmū (2 lbs. ea.), cleaned and scaled
2 cups	all-purpose flour
1 tbsp.	ground anise seed (optional)
4 cups	kosher salt
1 cup	water

Preheat oven to 375-400 degrees. Combine flour, anise seed (optional) and salt in a large bowl. Add water and stir to form slightly stiff dough. Let rest 1/2 hour. Rinse kūmū and pat dry. Lightly oil the bottom of a baking pan large enough to hold the individual fish. Spread dough out 1/4-in. thick over the bottom of the dish in the shape of the fish. Place the fish on top of the dough, then pat the rest of the dough around the sides and top of the fish to cover it completely. Bake in a 375-400 degree oven until golden brown. (A 2-lb. fish takes 30-40 minutes.) To serve, gently crack the salt crust, which will have hardened during baking so it will break into chunks. After removing salt crust, gently carve out fillets of fish and place on a plate. Spoon on Tomato Edamame Relish. Serves 4-6. (Note: The crust is not edible. It is used for flavoring and to hold in the steam.)

Tomato Edamame Relish

1 cup	diced tomatoes
1/2 cup	edamame (soy beans)
2 tbsp.	diced yellow onion
2 tbsp.	sliced green onion
1/2 tbsp.	chili pepper water
	salt and pepper to taste

Combine ingredients and mix well.

Recommended wine: Fumé Blanc

PAN-SEARED MOANO ON WARM WATERCRESS AND SWEET CORN BROTH

Both watercress and fish share centerpiece honors in this attractive and delightfully tasty dish.

6	4-oz. moano fillets (from 3 10- to 12-oz. whole fish)
2 tbsp.	salad oil
	salt and pepper to taste

In a sauté pan, heat oil until it starts to smoke. Sear fillets 2 minutes on each side.

Sweet Corn Broth

1-1/2 cups	corn kernels
3 cups	clam juice (may substitute Basic Fish Stock; see Basic Recipes)
1/2 tsp.	turmeric
6 oz.	unsalted butter (cut into pieces)
	salt and pepper to taste

Bring 1 cup corn, clam juice and turmeric to a boil. Let stand 2 minutes. Pour into a blender. Blend and add butter piece-by-piece. Season with salt and pepper; strain. Add remaining 1/2 cup of corn to broth.

Warm Watercress

3 cups	watercress
2 tbsp.	red onions, thinly sliced
1 tbsp.	salad oil
	salt and pepper to taste

Sauté watercress and red onions in oil until slightly wilted. Season with salt and pepper. Place in center of plate and pour corn broth around the watercress. Place sautéed moano fillets over watercress. Garnish with a sprig of watercress. Serves 4-6.

Recommended wines: Fumé Blanc, Sauvignon Blanc

BANANA LEAF-WRAPPED MOANO WITH COCONUT CRAB-SPINACH FILLING

Using banana leaf as a wrap adds a unique flavor to this dish, but ti leaf or foil may be substituted.

6	3-oz. moano fillets (from 3 10- to 12-oz. fish)
2 tbsp.	salad oil
3 tbsp.	minced onions
1/2 tsp.	minced garlic
1 cup	coconut milk
1 tsp.	cornstarch mix (dissolved in 1/4 cup water)
	salt and pepper to taste
1 cup	chopped fresh spinach
4 oz.	blue crab meat (may substitute chopped shrimp or lobster)
6	5x6-in. banana leaves (wave leaves over burner on stove until oil starts coming out and leaf becomes pliable)

Heat oil to medium; sauté onions and garlic 2 minutes, until translucent. Pour in coconut milk and simmer until liquid is reduced by half. Thicken with cornstarch mixture and season with salt and pepper. Fold in spinach and crabmeat. Place a dollop of the crab-spinach mixture in the center of each banana leaf, top with a fish fillet and another dollop of crab-spinach mixture. Fold the bottom of the leaf to the center, followed by the top and sides. Place each bundle upside-down (with the flaps down) in a bamboo steamer over boiling water. Steam 20-25 minutes until done. Serves 4-6.

Recommended wines: Fumé Blanc, Sauvignon Blanc

PAN-SEARED MOANO ON CHILLED SOMEN SALAD WITH KAFFIR LIME SESAME SEED DRESSING

Here's a great summertime dish that's light and flavorful. You can also try this dish with sweet blue crab meat.

6	moano fillets (3 oz. ea., from 3 10- to 12-oz. whole fish)
	Seasoned Flour (see Basic Recipes)
2 tbsp.	salad oil
2 cups	cooked somen noodles
1/2 cup	julienned cucumber
1/4 cup	julienned red onion
1/2 cup	julienned fish cake
	salt and pepper to taste
	julienned nori strips (optional)

Dredge fillets in seasoned flour and shake off excess. In a sauté pan, bring oil to medium heat. Sear fillets 3-4 minutes on each side. Combine remaining ingredients in a bowl and toss with 1 cup of kaffir lime sesame dressing. Serve fish over salad. Serves 4-6.

Kaffir Lime Sesame Seed Dressing

5	kaffir lime leaves, finely julienned
1/4 cup	orange juice concentrate
1/2 tsp.	minced garllic
1/2 tsp.	minced ginger
1 tbsp.	toasted sesame seeds
1/8 cup 1/2 tbsp.	sugar
1/2 cup	minced yellow onion
1/3 cup	rice wine vinegar
1 cup	salad oil
1/4 cup	water

Combine all ingredients except oil and water. Slowly whisk in oil. (If dressing is too thick, dilute with water until you have a desirable consistency.) Yields 2 cups.

Recommended wine: Johannisberg Riesling

The spiciness of the peanut sauce adds a nutty flavor to this baked fish dish.

1	whole weke (16-20 oz.)
2 tbsp.	finely minced ginger
2	finely minced lemongrass stalks
2	finely minced kaffir lime leaves
2 tsp.	minced garlic
1 tbsp.	Basic Herb Oil (see Basic Recipes)
1 tsp.	crushed red chili flakes

Score weke on both sides. Combine remaining ingredients and rub mixture all over the fish, including the cavity. Marinate 2 hours. Preheat oven to 425 degrees. Place fish on a well-oiled sheet pan. Bake 20-25 minutes. Serve with Spicy Peanut Sauce on side. Serves 2-3.

Spicy Peanut Sauce

1 cup	coconut milk
1 cup	water
1/2 lb.	peanut butter
1/4 cup	roughly chopped lemongrass
1/4 cup	roughly chopped ginger
1/4 cup	minced garlic
1/4 cup	garlic chili sauce
1/4 cup	granulated sugar
2 tsp.	chicken base
1	kaffir lime leaf
	salt and pepper to taste

In a pot, combine all ingredients, except salt and pepper. Bring to a boil. Season with salt and pepper. Simmer 10-15 minutes and strain.

Recommended wines: Johannisberg Riesling, White Zinfandel

OLIVE OIL-POACHED WEKE 'ULA WITH ARTICHOKE OLIVE SALAD, BASIL OIL AND BALSAMIC SYRUP

In Chinatown, it's not unusual to find beautiful, petite (3-4 oz.) whole red weke. Rather than pan-frying this fish, poach it in olive oil to give it a buttery texture.

6	whole red weke 'ula (red goatfish, 3-4 oz. ea.), scored
4 cups	extra virgin olive oil
	salt and pepper to taste

Preheat olive oil to 160 degrees. Season fish with salt and pepper. Place in heated oil and poach 7-8 minutes. (Note: If the fish is not submerged, baste it until done.) Place fish on top of artichoke salad; drizzle with basil oil and balsamic syrup (2 cups balsamic vinegar, heated until reduced by half, then chilled). Serves 4-6.

Basil Oil

1/4 cup	salad oil
1 cup	basil leaves

Pour oil over basil leaves. Blend in a blender for 2 minutes. Strain.

Artichoke Olive Salad

4 cups	artichoke quarters
3 tbsp.	red onions, thinly sliced
1/2 cup	sliced olives
1 tsp.	minced garlic
1 tbsp.	julienned basil leaves
1 tbsp.	sliced sundried tomatoes
	juice of 1/2 lemon
	salt and pepper to taste

Combine all ingredients in a bowl and lightly toss with basil oil.

Recommended wines: Fumé Blanc, Sauvignon Blanc

ISO PEANUT-CRUSTED WHITE WEKE WITH TRUFFLEYAKI SAUCE

The crunchy and crusty coating adds texture to the weke, which is richly seasoned with truffle mushroom peelings and teriyaki sauce.

8	white weke fillets (4 oz. ea., from 4 1-lb. whole fish)
1 cup	ground iso peanuts
1 cup	panko
1/4 cup	salad oil
	salt and pepper to taste

Combine iso peanuts and panko. Dredge skin side of weke fillets in this mixture. In a sauté pan, heat oil and sear fish on crusted side 2-3 minutes. Sear the other side another 2-3 minutes. Top with sauce. Good served with potato-macaroni salad. Serves 6-8.

Truffleyaki Sauce

1 cup	Basic Teriyaki Sauce (see Basic Recipes)
1 tbsp.	truffle peelings
1/2 tbsp.	truffle oil
2 oz.	unsalted butter

Place teriyaki in blender and blend with truffle peeling and truffle oil while slowly adding unsalted butter until well-incorporated. (This creates a creamier sauce.)

Recommended wine: Johannisberg Riesling

ESCABECHE OF WEKE 'ULA (PICKLED FISH)

Escabeche is one of those dishes that you can prepare one or two days ahead of time. Escabeche, of Cuban origin, is a pickled or marinated fish. The fish is fried first, then marinated in oil and vinegar and left out at room temperature.

6-8	whole weke 'ula (red goatfish, 3 oz. ea.)
	salt and pepper to taste
	juice of I lime
	flour for dredging
3 cups	olive oil
3	large onions sliced
2	large green bell peppers, seeded and cut into 1/4-in. strips
8	cloves crushed garlic
I cup	pitted kalamata olives
2 tsp.	crushed chili flakes
10	black whole peppercorns
I	bay leaf
I cup	white vinegar

Season whole fish with salt, pepper and lime juice. Allow to marinate I hour. Pat dry and dredge lightly in flour. In a medium sauté pan, heat I cup of olive oil until fragrant. Lightly brown fish 2-3 minutes on each side. Place fish in a large bowl; cool completely. In a medium-sized saucepan, heat the remaining oil over medium heat until fragrant. Add onions, bell peppers and garlic; cook until tender. Reduce heat to low and add olives, crushed chili flakes, peppercorns and bay leaf. Cook another 5 minutes, stirring occasionally. Add vinegar and cook until the mixture reaches a gentle boil. Remove from heat and cool completely. Pour cooled mixture over the fish. Cover or wrap tightly in cellophane or foil. Allow to marinate for I-2 days in a cool place, 70-75-degrees. Refrigeration is the next best option. To serve, re-season mixture and serve with crusty bread. Serves 4-6.

Recommended wines: Fumé Blanc, Sauvignon Blanc

EXTRA CRISPY 'OAMA WITH HAWAIIAN CHILI PEPPER REMOULADE DIP

Everyone in New Orleans has a version of remoulade, a condiment with both zing and creaminess. I use Hawaiian chili peppers to give my remoulade an island twist.

8	whole 'oama (up to 7 in. ea.)
4 cups	salad oil
	Seasoned Flour (see Basic Recipes)
	salt and pepper to taste
	Hawaiian Chili Pepper Remoulade (see Basic Recipes)

Preheat oil to 350 degrees in medium pan. Oil is ready when a pinch of Seasoned Flour sizzles when sprinkled over the oil. Dredge 'oama in Seasoned Flour and shake off excess. Deep-fry 6 minutes or until crispy. Drain on paper towels. Serve with Remoulade. Serves 4.

Recommended wine: Johannisberg Riesling

TEMPURA FRIED 'OAMA WITH SPICY KOREAN SAUCE

This dish, reminiscent of a traditional Korean chicken dish with a spicy sauce, substitutes fish tempura for the chicken.

12	whole 'oama (7 in. or smaller)
4 cups	salad oil
	Seasoned Flour (see Basic Recipes)
	Tempura Batter (see Basic Recipes)
	toasted sesame seeds, for garnish
	sliced green onions, for garnish

Preheat oil to 325 degrees. (Oil is ready when a pinch of seasoned flour sizzles when sprinkled over the oil.) Dredge 'oama in Seasoned Flour; shake off excess. Dip in Tempura Batter. Deep-fry for 4-6 minutes or until golden brown. Drain on paper towels. Toss 'oama with Spicy Korean Sauce to coat. Garnish with toasted sesame seeds and green onions. Serve immediately. Serves 4-6.

Spicy Korean Sauce

3 tbsp.	minced ginger
1 tbsp.	minced garlic
1/2 tbsp.	sesame oil
3 tbsp.	toasted white sesame seeds
1 cup	soy sauce
2 cups	sugar
2 tbsp.	sliced green onion
1/2 cup	garlic chili sauce
1-1/2 cups	water
	slurry (3 tbsp. cornstarch dissolved in 2 oz. water, mixed well)

Combine all ingredients except slurry in a pot. Bring to a boil. Thicken with slurry to desired consistency. Serve at room temperature.

Recommended wine: Johannisberg Riesling

GROUPER

GROUPERS

Hāpu'upu'u • Roi

This section will show you how to become familiar with and prepare two types of groupers: Hawaiian seabass (hāpu'upu'u) and peacock grouper (roi). Both are commonly found in Hawaiian waters and are also easily obtainable at local fish markets. The roi seabass was introduced into Hawai'i from Moorea in 1956. Don't be alarmed when you learn that this particular fish is associated with ciguatera. Actually, only the larger fish have caused this strain of fish poisoning. But before purchasing a fish, be sure to ask your fishmonger if it's been tested for ciguatera. Both of these groupers have medium textured flesh and are delicate to moderate in flavor. The flesh can withstand lots of tossing and stirring, as in the preparation of chowder, jambalaya and bowtie pasta. That's a big plus, because it won't crumble and disappear into the sauce.

HĀPUʻUPUʻU BEIGNET

During our three-year stay in New Orleans, my wife, Samantha, and I visited Cafe au Monde once a week. The cafe served only coffee and beignet, a light fluffy doughnut dusted with loads of powdered sugar (similar to malassadas). The version here is excellent with Basic Hawaiian Chili Pepper Remoulade.

I lb.	hāpuʻupuʻu, diced in large pieces (from a 3-lb. whole fish)
I qt.	salad oil

Beignet Batter

I-1/2 cups	flour
1/2 cup	masa harina (ground cornmeal)
3	eggs
I tbsp.	baking powder
3 cups	milk
1/2 cup	diced onion
1/4 cup	diced red bell pepper
1/4 cup	diced celery
I tsp.	minced garlic
I tbsp.	Worcestershire sauce
1/2 cup	salad oil
3/4 tbsp.	Tabasco sauce
2 tbsp.	Chef E Spice (see Basic Recipes)

Combine first 5 ingredients until smooth; set aside. Sauté vegetables for 3 minutes over medium heat. Let cool. Fold cooled sautéed ingredients into flour mixture. Add remaining ingredients and mix well. (This basic batter is very versatile and can be used with shellfish, firm island fish, poultry, vegetables and more). Fold in hāpuʻupuʻu, raw or cooked. Heat salad oil to 325 to 350 degrees. Use a I oz. scoop to scoop batter into hot oil. Fry 4-5 minutes, until beignet floats to the surface. Drain on paper towels and season with salt and pepper. Best served when hot with Basic Hawaiian Chili Pepper Remoulade (see Basic Recipes). Serves 6 to 8.

Recommended wine: Pinot Grigio

SPICED PUMPKIN SEED-DUSTED HĀPU'UPU'U WITH OKINAWAN MASHED POTATOES

Spiced pumpkin seeds give this dish some kick and a nice crunchy texture.

6	hāpu'upu'u fillets (4 oz. ea.)
	salt and pepper to taste
1 tbsp.	Chef E Spice (see Basic Recipes)
4 tbsp.	unsalted pumpkin seeds
1/4 cup	vegetable oil

Preheat oven to 400 degrees. Combine Chef E Spice and pumpkin seeds in a coffee grinder and coarsely grind. Transfer to a platter. Season fillets with salt and pepper, then firmly press one side into the seed mixture. Heat oil in a sauté pan and sear coated side for 2 minutes. Turn fillet and sear the other side for 2 minutes. Transfer fish to a baking pan and place in the oven for 5 minutes. Serve with Okinawan Mashed Potatoes. Serves 4-6.

Okinawan Mashed Potatoes

1-1/2 lbs.	Okinawan sweet potatoes, peeled and cubed
1 qt.	heavy cream
6 tbsp.	butter, at room temperature
	salt and pepper to taste

Place potatoes in a pot of water; bring to boil. Reduce heat and simmer for 20-30 minutes until tender. Drain. Mash potatoes with a potato masher or whisk. Meanwhile, bring cream to a boil. Add butter, 1 tbsp. at a time, to potatoes, and add cream gradually to achieve the desired texture. Season with salt and pepper; keep warm.

Recommended wine: Pinot Grigio

POOR MAN'S CRAB-CRUSTED HĀPUʻUPUʻU ON WARM SPINACH/FRISEE WITH TOASTED MACADAMIA NUT VINAIGRETTE

The spiciness of the crab crust complements the baked fish.

6	hāpuʻupuʻu fillets
	salt and pepper to taste
I cup	spinach
I cup	frisee
I tbsp.	macadamia nut oil

Bring macadamia nut oil to moderate heat and quickly sauté spinach and frisee for I minute until slightly wilted; season.

Imitation Crab Crust

10 oz.	imitation crab (may substitute snow crab or blue crab meat)
6 tbsp.	mayonnaise
I tbsp.	horseradish
2 tsp.	minced chives
4 tsp.	minced onions
	juice from 1/2 lemon

Preheat oven to 325 degrees. Combine crust ingredients and mix well. Season fillets with salt and pepper. Top fillets with crab crust and place on baking sheet. Bake 10-15 minutes. Serve fillets on a bed of sautéed spinach and frisee (as above). Drizzle with Toasted Macadamia Nut Vinaigrette.

Toasted Macadamia Nut Vinaigrette

1/3 cup	macadamia nut oil
1/3 cup	sugar
1/3 cup	rice wine vinegar
1 tbsp.	orange juice concentrate
3	kaffir lime leaves, finely julienned
1/4 tsp.	minced garlic
4 tbsp.	toasted macadamia nuts
	salt and pepper to taste

Combine all ingredients except macadamia nuts, salt and pepper. Let sit for 1 hour, then strain. Add nuts and season with salt and pepper.

Recommended wine: Chardonnay

BRAISED HĀPUʻUPUʻU IN RED THAI CURRY SAUCE

This dish is great for cold winter nights. Red Thai curry is guaranteed to warm you up.

6	hāpuʻupuʻu fillets (5 oz. ea.)
l tbsp.	salad oil
	salt and pepper to taste

Heat oil in a sauté pan and sear fillets for 2 minutes per side. Season with salt and pepper. Set aside.

Red Thai Curry Sauce

2 tsp.	salad oil
l tbsp.	minced garlic
l tbsp.	minced ginger
l tbsp.	minced lemongrass
l tbsp.	red Thai curry paste
l tbsp.	fish sauce
l cup	chicken stock (may substitute water)
3 ea.	kaffir lime leaves (may substitute lime zest)
1/2 cup	heavy cream
2 cups	coconut milk
	salt and pepper to taste
1/2 cup	cornstarch whisked in water to the consistency of heavy cream

Heat oil in sauté pan. Add garlic, ginger and lemongrass, then stir in curry paste. Cook 3 minutes, until light brown. Deglaze pan with fish sauce. Add stock and lime leaves. Reduce mixture by half. Add cream and coconut milk; season with salt and pepper. Thicken sauce with constarch slurry to desired thickness. Strain. Add seared fillets, then cover pan and simmer over low heat until fish is cooked through. Serves 4-6.

Recommended wines: Pinot Grigio, Johannisberg Riesling

ROI SEAFOOD CHOWDER

1 cup	diced bacon
1 cup	diced onions
1/2 cup	diced carrot
1/2 cup	diced celery
2 sprigs	thyme
1/2 tbsp.	minced garlic
6 cups	chicken stock
4 cups	clam juice
2 cups	coconut milk
2 cups	heavy cream
2 cups	fresh or frozen corn kernels
2	bay leaves
3 cups	diced Idaho potatoes
1-1/2 lbs.	seafood mix (clams, roi chunks, shrimp, mussels, etc.)

Cook bacon in a stock pot over low heat to render fat, 3-4 minutes. Add onions, carrots, celery, thyme and garlic. Cook until translucent, 3-4 minutes. Add chicken stock, clam juice, coconut milk, heavy cream, corn and bay leaves. Bring to a boil. Thicken to desired consistency with Blond Roux. Add thyme and potatoes; simmer 10 minutes. Add seafood mix; simmer 5 minutes, adjust seasonings. Serves 4-6.

Blond Roux

12 oz.	unsalted butter
1/2 lb.	flour

Melt butter in a saucepot. Add flour and stir until thoroughly mixed. Cook 5-8 minutes, until color darkens. (For use as a soup thickener, leave Roux a little runny so there won't be any clumps in the finished soup.)

Recommended wine: Chardonnay

ROI AND SHRIMP JAMBALAYA

This Louisiana-style jambalaya is filled with sausage, herbs and spices, and enhanced with roi seabass and shrimp.

6 oz.	roi fillet, cut in 1-in. cubes (from 1- to 1-1/2-lbs. whole fish)
4 oz.	butter
6 oz.	diced Portuguese sausage
1-1/2 cups	diced yellow onions
1-1/2 cups	diced celery
1 cup	diced green bell peppers
1-1/2 tsp.	minced garlic
4	bay leaves
2 tbsp.	Chef E Spice (see Basic Recipes)
2 cups	Uncle Ben's rice
4 cups	shrimp or chicken stock
4 oz.	31/40 black tiger shrimp
4 tbsp.	sliced green onions

In a heavy skillet, melt butter over high heat. Add sausage and cook
5 minutes. Add onions, celery, bell peppers, garlic, bay leaf and Chef E
Spice. Stir well and continue cooking 8-10 minutes, until browned.
Stir in rice and cook for 5 minutes, scraping the bottom of the pan
occasionally. Add stock, stirring well. Bring mixture to a boil, then
reduce heat and simmer 10 minutes. Add seafood and simmer
10 more minutes, stirring occasionally. Fold in green onions.

Recommended wines: Pinot Grigio, Johannisberg Riesling

BOWTIE PASTA TOSSED WITH ROI AND CLAM SCAMPI SAUCE

You'll love this garlicky scampi cream sauce tossed with pasta and seafood.

6 oz.	roi, cut in 1-in. cubes (from 1-1/2-lb. whole fish)
2 tsp.	salad oil
2 tbsp.	minced yellow onion
2 tsp.	chopped garlic
20 ea.	Manila clams
2 tbsp.	white wine
3 oz.	heavy cream
2 oz.	unsalted butter
2 tbsp.	diced tomato
2 tsp.	chopped parsley
	splash of Tabasco and Worcestershire sauces
	salt and pepper to taste
1 lb.	cooked bowtie pasta (farfalle)

Heat oil over medium heat and sauté onions, garlic, clams and roi for 3-4 minutes. Deglaze pan with white wine. Continue cooking until liquid is almost evaporated, then add heavy cream. When liquid is reduced by half, fold in butter. Add tomato, parsley, Tabasco and Worcestershire sauces. Season with salt and pepper.
Toss with pasta. Serves 4-6.

Recommended wine: Chardonnay

Jack and Trevally

Butaguchi • Ulua

Growing up in Hawai'i, I never realized there were so many species of jacks and trevally. Like many kama'aina, I was familiar only with papio and ulua. Papio is the juvenile version of ulua, usually weighing less than ten pounds, while the ulua weighs ten or more.

These are highly prized game fishes — not actually reef fishes — but I'm including them here anyway. These carnivores are silvery, strong swimmers that reside in the reef and often eat the reef fishes. At Sam Choy's Diamond Head, I've been fortunate to work with professional ulua fishermen who double as waiters. These guys know their fish, and I often buy their prize catch for the evening specials.

You'll find that several of these recipes call for butaguchi, a thick-lipped ulua. I highly recommend that you buy this fish if you ever get the opportunity. The flesh has a lot of fat, which makes it very buttery and ideal for raw food preparations.

TEMPURA SASHIMI BUTAGUCHI WITH TRUFFLED LIME SAUCE

This dish brings out the best flavors of this popular island fish. The crunchiness on the outside complements the buttery meat, which is further enhanced by the lime sauce.

5 blocks	butaguchi (3 oz. ea., from shoulder area of 10- to 15-lb. whole fish)
4 cups	salad oil
2 sheets	nori (seaweed) cut into thirds
	Seasoned Flour (see Basic Recipes)
	Tempura Batter (see Basic Recipes)
	salt and pepper to taste
	radish sprouts and wasabi, for garnish

Heat oil to 325 degrees. Season each butaguchi block with salt and pepper; wrap with nori strip. Dredge in seasoned flour and shake off excess. Dip fish in tempura batter and deep-fry until slightly golden, 1-2 minutes. Season and slice immediately. Fish should be rare to medim-rare. Serve with Truffled Lime Sauce and garnish with radish sprouts and a ball of wasabi. Serves 4-6.

Truffled Lime Sauce

2 tbsp.	lime sauce
1 tbsp.	mirin
2 tbsp.	sugar
2 tbsp.	soy sauce
1 tbsp.	minced truffle peelings
1 tbsp.	truffle oil

Combine ingredients and use as a dipping sauce.

Recommended wine: Pinot Grigio

Butaguchi is a thick-lipped ulua that is high in fat. It tastes great eaten raw.

5	butaguchi, thinly sliced (3 oz. ea., from 4- to 6-lb. whole fish)
I cup	salad oil
I tbsp.	Asian Oil (see Basic Recipes)
I tbsp.	soy sauce
4 cups	hot cooked rice
3 tbsp.	Sushi Rice Liquid
12	fried won ton pi
I	whole avocado, sliced
	sweet chili sauce (optional)
	radish sprouts or julienned nori, for garnish

Heat oil until it is smoking. Meanwhile, arrange butaguchi slices on a sheet pan or plate. Spread Asian Oil over surface of fish. Drizzle with soy sauce. Carefully pour hot salad oil over fish. Set aside. Combine hot rice with Sushi Rice Liquid. Arrange won ton pi on a serving dish. Top with a layer of sushi rice 1/4-in. thick. Follow with a layer of avocado slices. Drizzle with sweet chili sauce, then add a layer of seared butaguchi. Garnish with radish sprouts or julienned nori. Serves 4-6.

Sushi Rice Liquid

2 cups	rice vinegar
I cup	sugar
1/4 cup	salt
2 pieces	dashi konbu (dried kelp)

Combine ingredients and mix well.

Recommended wine: Pinot Grigio

Grilled corn adds a distinct smoky flavor to the relish that complements this dish.

4	butaguchi fillets (5 oz. ea., from 5- to 6-lb. whole fish)
1/4 cup	Basic Herb Oil (see Basic Recipes)
	salt and pepper to taste
	Basic Garlic Butter (see Basic Recipes)

Marinate fillets in herb oil for 10 to 15 minutes. Season with salt and pepper. Grill 3-4 minutes on each side. Top each fillet with a dollop of Basic Garlic Butter. Serve with relish. Serves 4-6.

Charred Jalapeno Corn Relish

2 cups	charred corn kernels (grill 4 ears of shucked corn 5-10 minutes, turning periodically)
1/2 cup	diced red bell peppers
1/2 cup	diced red onions
1 cup	sliced green onions
2	minced jalapenos
1 cup	mayonnaise
	juice of 1/2 lemon
	minced cilantro (optional)

Combine all ingredients and chill.

Recommended wine: Pinot Grigio

GRILLED HOISIN BBQ ULUA

4   white ulua fillets (5 oz. ea., from 5- to 6-lb. whole fish)
2 cups   Hoisin BBQ Sauce

Marinate fillets in Hoisin BBQ sauce for 1 hour. Grill 3 minutes per side, brushing periodically with BBQ Sauce. Serve with grilled vegetables. Serves 4-6.

Hoisin BBQ Sauce

1 cup   hoisin sauce
1/2 cup   ketchup
3 tbsp.   granulated sugar
1/4 cup   water
1 tbsp.   sesame oil
1/2 tbsp.   toasted sesame seeds
1/4 cup   salad oil
1 tbsp.   chili-garlic sauce
1/2 tbsp.   minced garlic
2 tbsp.   ginger juice

Combine all ingredients and mix well.

Recommended wines: Pinot Grigio, Johannisberg Riesling

HONEY MACADAMIA NUT-CRUSTED ULUA

| 4 | ulua fillets (5 oz. ea., from 5- to 6-lb. whole fish) |
| | salt and pepper to taste |

Honey Macadamia Nut Crust

1/3 cup	honey
1/2 tbsp.	minced thyme
1/2 tbsp.	minced garlic
1/2 tbsp.	Pommery mustard
	(may substitute Dijon or Creole mustard)
1/4 tsp.	salt
2 turns	cracked black pepper
2 cups	crushed toasted macadamia nuts
	(may substitute any type of nuts)

Preheat oven to 325 degrees. To make crust, combine all ingredients except nuts and mix well. Fold in nuts and stir until well-coated. Season fish on both sides with salt and pepper. Spread a thin layer of the crust on top of each fillet. Place on a well-oiled baking pan. Bake 15-20 minutes (if fish is cooked through but crust is not yet golden, set oven on broil to brown crust). Serves 4-6.

Recommended wine: Chardonnay

KATAIFI-WRAPPED ULUA WITH SWEET-SOUR PAPAYA SAUCE

Kataifi is shredded phyllo. Using it as a wrapper gives the ulua a wonderful crispy texture.

12	ulua fingers (2 in. ea.)
	salt and pepper to taste
1 box	kataifi (shredded phyllo dough, found in specialty stores)
4 cups	salad oil

Season fish fingers with salt and pepper. Wrap each finger in kataifi dough.

Heat oil to 350 degrees. Fry fish for 3-5 minutes, until golden brown. Drain on paper towels and season wth more salt and pepper. Serve with Sweet and Sour Papaya Sauce. Serves 4-6.

Sweet and Sour Papaya Sauce

1/2 cup	sugar
1/2 cup	rice vinegar
1/2 cup	water
2 tbsp.	cornstarch
1-1/2 cups	pureed ripe papaya
	salt to taste

Place sugar, vinegar and water in a pot and bring to a boil. Thicken with cornstarch and mix to desired consistency. Cool for 30-45 minutes. Fold in papaya puree. Season with salt and pepper. Serve at room temperature.

Recommended wines: Pinot Grigio, Johannisberg Riesling

BLACK & WHITE SESAME SEED-PRESSED ULUA ON CRISPY TEMPURA VEGETABLES WITH SWEET WASABI SAUCE

6 pieces	white ulua (3-oz. fillets)
	salt and pepper to taste
1 tbsp.	black sesame seeds
1 tbsp.	white sesame seeds

Lay fish flat and season with salt and pepper. Press sesame seeds evenly onto fish. In a hot pan, cook fish until golden brown on each side. Serve with Vegetable Tempura, with Sweet Wasabi Sauce on the side. Serves 4-6.

Vegetable Tempura

2 cups	salad oil, for deep-frying
1 cup	Seasoned Flour (see Basic Recipes)
1 tsp.	salt
1/2 tsp.	pepper
1 cup	julienned carrots
1 bunch	watercress, cut in 1-in. pieces
1 cup	sliced onions
	Tempura Batter (see Basic Recipes)

Heat oil to 325-350 degrees. Combine flour, salt and pepper. Coat vegetables in Seasoned Flour. Dredge in tempura batter. Fry vegetables until golden brown. Drain on paper towels.

Sweet Wasabi Sauce

1/4 cup	minced shallots
1/2 cup	white wine
1/4 tsp.	minced garlic
1 sprig	thyme
	juice of 1 lemon
1	bay leaf
3	whole black peppercorns
1/3 cup	heavy cream
8 oz.	cold butter, diced
1/2 cup	wasabi paste
2 tbsp.	honey

In a pot, combine shallots, white wine, garlic, thyme, lemon, bay leaf and black peppercorns. Bring to a boil, then reduce heat and simmer until mixture is almost dry. Add cream and reduce by half. Whisk in butter until incorporated. Add wasabi paste and honey; simmer 10 minutes. Strain.

Recommended wine: Pinot Grigio

MULLET

MULLET

'Awa'awa

Mullet, or 'awa'awa, is a fish that many local cooks insist on steaming. It has a long body with a blunt snout, flattened head and large scales. A bottom feeder in sand or mud, the mullet can thrive in brackish water. Don't confuse this fish with the more expensive moi. (That's no exaggeration; moi is usually about $2 more per pound!) Following are a couple of dishes that use moist heat cooking to prepare mullet. You can also use the entire fish by steaming it Chinese-style. Also, for a pleasant surprise, try it as a whole roasted fish smothered with Basic Garlic Butter.

POACHED MULLET IN CHISO FENNEL BROTH

Clams, shrimp, mussels and other seafood can be added to this dish.

Chiso Fennel Broth

4-6	mullet fillets (3 oz. ea., from 3- to 4-lb. whole fish)
2 tbsp.	salad oil
2 cups	sliced yellow onion
2 cups	sliced fennel
2 tsp.	minced garlic
1/4 cup	julienned ginger
	pinch saffron threads
1/2 cup	Pernod or white wine
2 qt.	fish stock
12	julienned chiso leaves

Heat oil over medium heat. Cook onions and fennel 4-5 minutes, until tender. Add garlic and ginger; cook another 2 minutes. Add saffron and deglaze with wine. Cook until liquid is reduced by half. Add stock and bring to a boil. Reduce to a simmer. Add chiso and mullet; poach for 3-4 minutes, and season. Serves 4-6.

Recommended wine: Pinot Grigio

STEAMED STRIPED MULLET WITH BABY BOK CHOY AND LEMONGRASS-SCENTED SHELLFISH JUS

4-6	mullet fillets (3 oz., from 3- to 4-lb. whole fish)
1-1/2 to 2 lbs.	baby bok choy, quartered
	salt and pepper to taste

Place baby bok choy in bottom of a bamboo steamer basket. Place fillets on top of bok choy. Season with salt and pepper. Steam 8-10 minutes and set aside.

Lemongrass Scented Shellfish Jus

2 cups	Shellfish Stock (see Basic Recipes)
1/4 cup	minced lemongrass (from bottom 3 in. of lemongrass stalk)
6 oz.	unsalted butter (cut into pieces)
	salt and pepper to taste

Heat stock over low heat. Steep lemongrass in stock for 10 minutes. Puree hot liquid in blender, adding butter piece-by-piece. Season with salt and pepper. Place baby bok choy in the center of a bowl. Pour the sauce over the vegetables; top with fish. Serve with steamed rice. Serves 4-6.

Recommended wine: Johannisberg Riesling

PARROTFISH

Uhu

My father used to buy parrotfish, better known in the Islands as uhu, from local fishermen, who visited us weekly to sell their catch. He would buy enough to last our family two or three days, since uhu is such a versatile fish. You can prepare it in many very different ways — in keleguen, for instance, the Guamanian version of ceviche, or wrapped in foil with Asian ingredients, or simply cooked on your hibachi.

You can't miss a parrotfish at the store. It really stands out with its bluish-green color and that distinctive beak that lets it scrape and grind the algae on coral. Believe it or not, this is also one of the few species of fish that reverses its gender from female to male. It's also a major producer of sand in coral reef areas.

Parrotfish has a moderate flavor and a tender texture. When you're shopping for one, look for a two-to three-pounder for whole-use preparation or a larger one for great filleting.

UHU KELEGUEN

This Guamanian version of ceviche is very versatile. It can be served as an appetizer, salad or entree.

1 lb.	diced uhu
1/2 cup	minced onions
1/2 cup	sliced green onions
2 tbsp.	grated fresh coconut
3	minced Hawaiian chili peppers
1/3 cup	coconut milk
1/2 lb.	bay scallops (optional)
1/2 lb.	shrimp (optional)
	juice of 4 lemons
	juice of 3 limes
	salt and pepper to taste

Combine all ingredients and chill for 1-1/2 hours before serving.

Recommended wine: Fumé Blanc

This easy-to-prepare dish can go right from the oven to the table in its foil container.

4-5 lbs.	whole uhu
	salt and pepper to taste
1 cup	mayonnaise
4 oz.	sliced Portuguese sausage
1	sliced lemon
1	sliced medium onion
1	ti leaf
1 sheet	foil, large enough to wrap fish
1/4 cup	minced ginger
1 cup	chopped cilantro
1 cup	sliced green onion
6 tbsp.	soy sauce
2 tbsp.	sesame oil

Preheat oven to 350 degrees. Score fish 1 in. apart, cutting all the way to the bone, creating 1-in. diamonds on both sides. Season inside and out with salt and pepper. Rub mayonnaise in the score marks and cavity. Tuck sausage, lemon and sliced onion in the score marks. Place ti leaf in the center of foil sheet. Place fish on ti leaf. Sprinkle remaining ingredients evenly over fish. Gather edges of foil to the center and crimp tight to prevent steam from escaping. Bake 45 minutes to 1 hour. Serves 4-6.

Recommended wines: Fumé Blanc, Sauvignon Blanc

PORTUGUESE CRUSTED UHU WITH CREOLE MEUNIERE SAUCE

This recipe is a direct result of my experience working with Chef Emeril Lagasse, who taught me about the rich culinary traditions of the people of Louisiana, and about their many contributions to American cuisine.

6	uhu fillets (3 oz., from 3- to 4-lb. whole fish)
	salt and pepper to taste

Portuguese Sausage Crust

1/2 lb.	minced Portuguese sausage
	(may substitute any smoked sausage)
1 tbsp.	salad oil
1/4 cup	minced onions
1/4 cup	minced celery
1/4 cup	minced green bell pepper
1 tsp.	minced garlic
1/2 tbsp.	Chef E Spice (see Basic Recipes)
1/2 cup	sliced green onions
1/4 cup	grated Parmesan cheese
1	egg, beaten
2-1/2 cups	panko

To make crust: Cook sausage in oil over medium heat until fat is rendered, 3-5 minutes. Add onions, celery and bell pepper; cook until translucent. Add garlic, Chef E Spice and green onions. Remove from heat, fold in Parmesan cheese and chill. Once chilled, fold egg and panko into crust mixture. Preheat oven to 350 degrees. Season fish with salt and pepper. Sear each side in a hot pan for 1 minute. Place fillets on a baking sheet and spread Portuguese sausage crust on top of each one. Bake for 10-15 minutes until done. Serve over a pool of Creole Meuniere Sauce. Serves 4-6.

Creole Meuniere Sauce

1/2 tbsp.	minced shallots
1/2 tbsp.	minced garlic
1 cup	Worcestershire sauce
1/2 cup	white wine
1/4 cup	meat stock
1 cup	heavy cream
1-1/2 lb.	butter
	salt and pepper to taste

In a saucepan, combine first 5 ingredients and simmer until reduced by three-fourths. Add cream; reduce by half. Whisk in butter over low heat. Once all ingredients are incorporated, strain and season with salt and pepper.

Recommended wine: Chardonnay

SCAD

SCAD

Akule • ʻŌpelu

Scads are silvery blue-green fish. The most popular are the akule (big eye scad) and the ʻōpelu (mackerel scad, with a more elongated body).

Akule and ʻōpelu are easy to find. They're available at fishmarkets, local grocery stores and even from the folks who sell them at the side of the road in places like Waipahu. Because of their popularity, the price is always right. My father calls scad "the poor man's poke" because he and his friends use it in their shoyu poke. It's just as good as ʻahi, without the pocket expense. In Hawaiʻi you see a lot of the old-timers using "dry boxes" to air- and sun-dry akule and ʻōpelu, as well as aku (skipjack tuna) and sometimes marlin.

In this section, you'll learn how to cure and dry your own fish. I'll also show you how to prepare Poor Man's Poke, my dad's favorite.

DRIED 'ŌPELU

Add flavor to dried fish by brushing on your favorite teriyaki sauce hourly during the drying time. Add texture by sprinkling the fish with toasted sesame seeds.

5   whole 'ōpelu (1/2-1 lb. ea.)

Brine
1 gallon   water
2 cups   iodized salt

To butterfly 'ōpelu: Use a sharp knife to split fish from the dorsal fin at the top down to the pelvic (belly) area. Use the bone structure as a guide, but do not cut through. Clean the fish thoroughly, removing the gills and organs. Mix brine ingredients until salt is dissolved. Soak fish in brine for 2 hours for 1-lb. fish; 1-1/2 hours for 1/2-lb fish. Remove fish from brine and rinse thoroughly. Place in a drying box or wrap the fish lightly in cheesecloth and place it on a cooling rack. Dry in the sun 12-15 hours.

Recommended wine: White Zinfandel

6	whole 'ōpelu (4-5 oz. ea.)
12 oz.	Shrimp Hash
3 sheets	nori, cut in half
	salad oil for deep frying
	Tempura Batter (see Basic Recipes)
	Seasoned Flour (see Basic Recipes)
2 cups	ground uncooked shrimp chips

Remove heads from fish. Split in half, leaving tail attached. Clean and remove bones. Spread halves of the fish apart and stuff each fish with 2 oz. of shrimp hash. Wrap each fish with nori, leaving the tail sticking out at the end. Use tempura batter to seal nori. Heat salad oil to 350 degrees. Dredge stuffed 'ōpelu in Seasoned Flour, then dip in Tempura Batter. Drain excess batter. Roll 'ōpelu in ground shrimp chips. Deep fry for 4-6 minutes or until golden and crisp on the outside. Slice each fish into 3-4 bite-sized pieces. Serves 4-6.

Shrimp Hash

10 oz.	ground shrimp
1	egg
3 tbsp.	water chestnuts
2 tsp.	minced garlic
2 tbsp.	sliced green onion
1 tbsp.	oyster sauce
1/8 tsp.	sesame oil
	salt and pepper to taste

Combine all ingredients and chill.

Recommended wine: Chardonnay

DRIED 'ŌPELU WATERCRESS SOUP

This dish combines many flavors to create a light but satisfying soup to warm up your day — especially good on a cold morning!

1 lb.	dried 'ōpelu, bones removed and diced
1 tbsp.	salad oil
3 cloves	minced garlic
3/4 cup	sliced onions
2 tbsp.	fish sauce
32 oz.	chicken broth
2-in. finger	ginger, smashed
3/4 cup	watercress stems
3/4 cup	watercress tops
	salt and pepper to taste

Heat oil in a medium-sized pot. Sauté fish for 2 minutes. Add garlic and onions and sauté for 3 minutes over medium heat. Deglaze with fish sauce, then add chicken broth, ginger and watercress stems. Bring to boil, then reduce heat and simmer for 10 minutes. Skim soup. Just before serving, stir in the watercress tops and season with salt and pepper. Serves 4-6.

Recommended wine: Fumé Blanc

6	whole akule, gutted (6 oz. ea.)
1/4 cup	Basic Herb Oil (see Basic Recipes)
	Hawaiian salt
	fresh cracked black pepper

Lightly coat akule in Basic Herb Oil. Marinate 30 minutes. Lightly season fish with Hawaiian salt and black pepper. Grill on hibachi for 5-8 minutes until done. Serves 4-6.

Recommended wine: Fumé Blanc

ISLAND-SYLE AKULE POKE

Poke is an island favorite that has become famous beyond Hawai'i's shores, thanks mostly to Chef Sam Choy. This recipe features all the basic poke ingredients, although akule is used instead of the usual tuna.

5	large akule in 1/2-in. cubes (remove skin and bones, but bloodline may be kept)
1/2 cup	sliced Maui onion
2	minced Hawaiian chili peppers
1/2 cup	sliced green onion
3/4 cup	chopped thick ogo or limu-kohu
	Hawaiian salt to taste
6 tbsp.	soy sauce (optional)

Combine all ingredients in a bowl and serve chilled. Serves 4.

Recommended wines: Fumé Blanc, White Zinfandel

SCORPIONFISH

SCORPIONFISH
Nohu

If you think the barracuda looks ugly and ferocious, wait until you see the scorpionfish, or nohu. A master of camouflage, the scorpionfish has a large head with sharp spines on its head and body. This fish wasn't designed to chase its prey around but instead to remain stationary, waiting in ambush for its meal. In the past, nohu was considered a rubbish fish and not suitable for consumption. Now, however, these moderately priced fish are sure to be gone from the market by the end of the day.

This fish can be used as one of the main components in preparing an authentic bouillabaisse. Nohu is also great in soups, broth dishes, and sometimes in sautéed food preparation because of its firm flesh. When cutting this fish, keep in mind that its sharp spines can pierce your hands and fingers. What's more, its disproportionate body can also make cutting more difficult. Better idea: Ask your fishmonger to fillet it for you.

4-5	nohu fillets (3 oz. ea., from 5- to 6-lbs. whole fish)
2 tbsp.	salad oil
1/2 cup	julienned yellow onions
8 cups	Aromatic Braising Broth
1 can	straw mushrooms, drained
1/2 cup	snow peas
1/2 cup	diced tomatoes
3 tbsp.	julienned Thai basil
	salt and pepper to taste

In a braising pan, heat oil until smoking. Place nohu in pan and sauté for 1 minute on each side until fish shows a hint of color. Drain excess oil and add onions. Sauté for 1 minute. Add broth, mushrooms, peas and tomatoes. Simmer for 6-8 minutes until nohu is tender. Just before serving, fold in basil and season with salt and pepper. Serves 4-6.

Aromatic Braising Broth

8 cups	Fish Stock (see Basic Recipes)
2 fingers	ginger, crushed
6	Hawaiian chili peppers, crushed
1	whole garlic head, cut in half
3 stalks	lemongrass
4	star anise
1/4 cup	fish sauce

Combine all ingredients in a stock pot. Bring to a boil, reduce heat and simmer for 10 minutes. Strain.

Recommended wine: Pinot Grigio

NOHU WITH CHINESE-STYLE PENNE PASTA

8-10	nohu cubes (1-1/2 oz. ea., from 5- to 6-lb. whole fish)
2 tbsp.	salad oil
1 tbsp.	minced ginger
1 tbsp.	minced garlic
1 tbsp.	fermented black beans, rinsed and minced
12 oz.	canned chopped tomatoes
3/4 cup	Basic Fish Stock (see Basic Recipes; may substitute chicken stock)
2 tbsp.	heavy cream
1 tbsp.	sugar
1/4 tsp.	chili flakes
1 lb.	cooked penne pasta
2 tbsp.	lightly packed chopped cilantro
	sliced lup cheong (sweet Chinese sausage), optional
	salt and pepper to taste
1/2 cup	Parmesan cheese, grated

Heat oil in a sauté pan over medium heat. Sear nohu cubes for 3 minutes. Add ginger, garlic and black beans; cook for 2 minutes but do not brown. Add tomatoes and simmer for 3-4 minutes. Add fish stock and cook for another 2-3 minutes. Add cream, sugar and chili flakes and cook for 2 minutes. Stir in pasta, cilantro and sausage, if using. Season with salt and pepper. Top with Parmesan cheese just before serving. Serves 4-6.

Recommended wine: Pinot Grigio

2-3 lbs.	nohu heads (chopped into 3-in. pieces)
1 finger	ginger, smashed
1	tomato, chopped
1	onion, sliced
1-2	tamarind pods, shelled
	juice of 1/2 lemon
	salt and pepper to taste
1 lb.	ong choi, in 3-in. pieces

Rinse nohu pieces in cold water. Place in a stock pot and cover with water. Bring to a boil, then reduce heat to a simmer. Skim surface. Add remaining ingredients, except ong choi, and simmer for 20-30 minutes. Add ong choi in the last 30 minutes of cooking time. Season with salt and pepper.

Recommended wine: Johannisberg Riesling

This traditional French bouillabaisse has an Asian flavor, with its hints of lemongrass and chiso. This dish is easy to prepare, despite the many ingredients. It is well worth the time and effort.

4-5 chunks	nohu (2 oz. ea., about 2 x 2 in., from 2 3- to 4-lb. whole fish)
3 tbs.	olive oil
I	yellow onion, cut in 1/2-in. pieces
2 stalks	celery, sliced diagonally
I tbs.	minced garlic
	pinch of saffron threads
2 tbs.	tomato paste
1/2 cup	dry white wine
1-1/2 cups	crushed tomatoes
6 cups	clam juice (may substitute Fish or Shrimp Stock from Basic Recipes)
I	bay leaf
4 stalks	lemongrass, smashed
2-in. piece	ginger, smashed
12	Manila clams
12	mussels
12	6/20 size shrimp, peeled and deveined
3 tbsp.	julienned chiso (may substitute basil)
I tsp.	crushed chili pepper flakes
2 tbsp.	sugar
	lobster tails and crab legs (optional)

In a large saucepan, heat oil and sauté onion and celery until soft but not browned. Add garlic and saffron; sauté for 2 minutes. Stir in tomato paste and cook for an additional minute. Deglaze with white wine, scraping any bits from the bottom of the pan. Simmer until liquid is reduced by half. Stir in crushed tomatoes, clam juice, bay leaf, lemongrass and ginger. Bring to a boil, then reduce heat and simmer for 15 minutes. Discard lemongrass and ginger. Add clams and mussels to hot broth. When they begin to open, add shrimp and fish and simmer for 3-5 minutes. When using the optional lobster and crab, add them with the shrimp and fish. Add chiso and red pepper flakes. Season with salt and pepper. Taste and add some or all of the sugar to adjust the acidity of the broth. Serves 4-6.

Spicy Rouille

1 cup	mayonnaise
1 tsp.	minced garlic
	togarashi (Japanese pepper powder) to taste
	water
	salt to taste

Combine first 3 ingredients and mix well, then add just enough water to make the sauce smooth. Season with salt. Drizzle over toasted French bread and use as a garnish for the bouillabaisse.

Recommended wines: Fumé Blanc, White Zinfandel

SNAPPER

SNAPPER
Taape • Toau

When I was growing up on Maui, family gatherings were frequent
and the menu always featured some kind of fish. These gatherings
usually consisted of 40 to 60 people, and everybody knows how
Hawai'i people love to eat! To avoid breaking the bank, taape (blue-
striped snapper) and toau (blacktail snapper) were considered the
best fish to serve. They were very inexpensive, especially since fishermen usually just gave taape away because they had so many of them.

These snappers are great to sauté and deep fry. Neither fish
originated in Hawai'i. Toau was introduced from Moorea in 1956,
while taape was brought to the Hawaiian Islands from the Marquesas
two years after that — both to stimulate Hawai'i's fishing industry.
Unfortunately, this effort failed, largely because taape has such low
commercial value.

6	toau fish fillets (3 oz. ea., from 3 8-oz. whole fish)
	salt and pepper to taste
6	chiso leaves
6	lumpia wrappers
3/4 cup	sautéed shiitake mushrooms in salad oil,
	seasoned and chilled
I	egg, beaten
	salad oil for deep frying

Season fillets with salt and pepper. Wrap each fillet in a chiso leaf and place on the corner of a lumpia wrapper. Place spoonful of shiitake mushrooms on top of fish. Fold the corners of the wrapper over the fillet and roll up tightly. Brush the top flap with egg wash and seal. Heat oil to 325 degrees. Fry lumpia until golden brown, 5-8 minutes. Place fried lumpia onto a paper towel and set Pickled Li Hing Mui Mango Sauce in a ramekin for dipping. Serves 4-6.

Pickled Li Hing Mui Mango Sauce

I stalk	lemongrass, smashed
2 tbsp.	granulated sugar
2 tbsp.	water
2 tbsp.	white vinegar
I-in. finger	ginger, smashed
1/8 tsp.	minced garlic
1/8 tsp.	chili garlic sauce
2-1/2 cups	mango peeled, seeded and finely julienned
1/4 tsp.	li hing mui powder

Combine all ingredients but mango and li hing mui powder and let sit for 2-3 hours. Strain. Fold in julienned mango and li hing mui powder.

Recommended wine: Johannisberg Riesling

PAN-FRIED TOAU WITH FRIED GARLIC EDAMAME SAUCE AND PEA SHOOT SALAD

The Edamame Sauce and Pea Shoot Salad make an excellent accompaniment to pan-fried toau.

8	toau fillets (10 oz. ea.)
	salt and pepper to taste
	Seasoned Flour (see Basic Recipes)
1 cup	salad oil

Season toau with salt and pepper and lightly dredge in seasoned flour. Heat oil in a sauté pan over medium heat. Sear fillets for 3 minutes on each side. Place seared toau on center of plate. Drizzle Fried Garlic Edamame Sauce around fish. Top fish with Pea Shoot Salad. Serves 4-6.

FRIED GARLIC EDAMAME SAUCE

5 tbsp.	soy sauce
1 tbsp.	oyster sauce
1 lb.	unsalted butter
1 tbsp.	Fried Garlic (see Basic Recipes)
1 tbsp.	edamame (soy beans)

Combine soy and oyster sauces in a small saucepan. Simmer, reducing sauce by a third. Slowly whisk in butter until incorporated. Sprinkle fried garlic and edamame over sauce.

PEA SHOOT SALAD

1/4 lb.	fresh pea shoots
2 tbsp.	red onions, thinly sliced
1/8 cup	grape tomatoes
1 pkg.	enoki mushrooms
	balsamic vinaigrette to taste
	(4:1 ratio of salad oil to balsamic vinegar)
2 tbsp.	grated Parmesan cheese

Combine vegetables in a bowl and toss with vinaigrette to coat slightly. Sprinkle with Parmesan cheese.

Recommended wines: Fumé Blanc, Pinot Grigio

4	whole toau (4 oz. ea.), scaled and gutted
8	Kahuku prawns (may substitute shrimp)
	Chef E Spice (see Basic Recipes)
	cracked black pepper to taste
1/4	cup salad oil
1/2 cup	New Orleans BBQ Base
1/4 cup	heavy cream
1 tbsp.	unsalted butter
	salt and pepper

Season both sides of fish and prawns with Chef E Spice and pepper. Heat oil over medium heat and sear toau for 3-4 minutes on one side. Turn fish and add prawns. Cook for another 3-4 minutes. Remove fish and set aside. When prawns are half-cooked, deglaze pan with BBQ Base. When liquid is reduced by a third, add cream. Bring to a boil, fold in butter and season with salt and pepper. Pour BBQ prawns and sauce over toau. Serve with bread. Serves 4.

New Orleans BBQ Base

1 tbsp.	salad oil
2-1/4 cups	prawn shells (may substitute shrimp or lobster shells)
1-1/4 cups	chopped onions
2	lemons, peeled
1	bay leaf
1-in. finger	ginger, sliced
1 cup	Worcestershire sauce
1/2 tbsp.	minced garlic
1-1/4 cups	water
1 tbsp.	cracked black pepper
1 tbsp.	Chef E Spice (see Basic Recipes)

In a stock pot, heat oil until smoking. Sauté shells for 3 minutes until toasted. Add onions and sauté for another 3 minutes. Add remaining ingredients. Bring to a boil, then reduce heat and simmer until liquid is reduced by half. Strain. (Note: Save all your shells from prawns and shrimp and freeze them. You can keep them in the freezer up to a year, using them as you need them in this New Orleans BBQ Base, which is also great with lobster, clams and mussels.)

Recommended wine: Johannisberg Riesling

TRADITIONAL TAAPE SABAO

This sabao, or soup, brings back memories of my childhood, when my mom used this preparation to make a simple but soothing Filipino soup dish.

4-6	cooked whole taape (4-5 oz. ea.)
2 tbsp.	salad oil
I cup	sliced onion
I tbsp.	minced garlic
3 tbsp.	fish sauce (patis)
2	tomatoes, cut into wedges
2-in. finger	ginger, smashed
4	cups water or fish stock

In a saucepot, heat oil over medium heat. Add onions and garlic. Cook for 4 minutes but do not brown. Deglaze with fish sauce, stirring for 2 minutes. Add tomatoes, pan-fried fish, smashed ginger and water. Simmer for 15-20 minutes. Serve with a bowl of rice. Serves 4-6.

Recommended wine: Johannisberg Riesling

PAN-FRIED TAAPE WITH SPICY SWEET CHILI SAUCE

4-6	whole taape (4-5 oz. ea.), scaled and gutted
4 cups	salad oil
	Seasoned Flour (see Basic Recipes)
	salt and pepper to taste

Heat salad oil to 350 degrees (oil is ready when a pinch of flour sizzles when sprinkled over surface of the oil). Dredge taape in seasoned flour and shake off excess. Fry for 5-6 minutes or until done. Drain on paper towels. Place fish in a medium bowl, season with salt and pepper and toss with spicy sweet chili sauce until nicely coated. Serve immediately. Serves 4-6.

Spicy Sweet Chili Sauce

1/2 tbsp.	soy sauce
1/2 tbsp	mustard powder
1-1/2 cups	Thai sweet chili sauce (available at Asian grocery stores)
1/2 tbsp.	black sesame seeds

Combine soy sauce and mustard to make a paste. Combine with remaining ingredients and mix well.

Recommended wines: Johannisberg Riesling, White Zinfandel

CASIAN-SPICED TAAPE WITH PAPAYA RELISH

Casian is my version of blackened fish — a blend of Cajun and Asian. Taape can withstand the bold spices and goes very well with the refreshing papaya relish.

4-6	whole taape (6 oz. ea.), scaled and gutted
	Chef E Spice (see Basic Recipes)
6 tbsp.	salad oil

Season fish moderately with Chef E Spice. Heat oil in sauté pan over medium heat. Cook fish 3-4 minutes on each side until done. Serve with Papaya Relish. Serves 4-6.

Papaya Relish

1	whole ripe papaya. skinned, seeded and diced
1/2 cup	diced red onion
1/4 cup	sliced green onion
	juice from 1/2 lime
2 tbsp.	salad oil
	salt and pepper to taste

Combine all ingredients and chill.

Recommended wine: Pinot Grigio

SURGEONFISH

Manini • Kala

Manini was my mother's favorite fish. She would prepare it whenever I came home to Maui. It's a hearty fish with lots of flavor, and she didn't have to do much except just scale and gut it. Manini can be enjoyed in a number of soups or broths. This fish is distinguished by its six vertical stripes, hence its other name — convict tang. It's robust in flavor and very affordable.

Kala can be enjoyed on the grill. This fish has a tough skin; in old Hawai'i it was used for drumheads. This skin creates a foil-like cover that holds in steam, which allows the fish to cook thoroughly on the grill. The kala's diet consists mainly of seaweed, and many people don't care for it because of the resultant fishy/seaweed flavor. In one of the following recipes, I use this seaweed taste in creating a poke dish. In another, I remove the skin and marinate the fish in a kalbi sauce.

1 lb.	cubed kala (from 2-lb. whole fish)
1/2 cup	sliced green onions
1/2 cup	minced yellow onions
	Hawaiian salt to taste
3 tbsp.	inamona (ground kukui nuts)
1 ea.	minced Hawaiian chili pepper
	limu-kohu (optional; be aware that kala already has a distinct seaweed taste)

Combine all ingredients and chill. Serves 4-6.

Recommended wine: Pinot Grigio

SEARED KALA

6	kala fillets (4 oz. ea., from 2-1/2-lb. whole fish)
2 tbsp.	salad oil
	salt and pepper to taste

Marinade

1 cup	soy sauce
1/4 cup	sesame oil
1-1/2 tbsp.	toasted sesame seeds
2 tbsp.	sliced green onion
2 tbsp.	minced yellow onion
4 tbsp.	brown sugar
2 tsp.	sriracha chili
1- to 2-in. finger	ginger, smashed

Combine marinade ingredients. Marinate fillets for 1-1/2 to 2 hours. In a saucepan, heat oil and sear kala 2-3 minutes on each side until done. Season with salt and pepper. Serves 4-6.

Recommended wine: Pinot Grigio

KOREAN KALBI KALA

This version of the traditional Korean favorite uses kala in place of short ribs.

4	whole kala (2 lb. ea.), cleaned but not scaled

Kalbi Marinade

2 tbsp.	sugar
1/2 cup	soy sauce
3 tbsp.	honey
6 cloves	garlic, smashed
1/4 cup	sliced green onion
2 tbsp.	sesame oil
1 tbsp.	toasted sesame oil
2 tsp.	minced ginger

Make a few holes in the fish. Combine marinade ingredients and mix well. Marinate fish for 4-6 hours. Grill for 15-20 minutes, turning occasionally. Serves 4-6.

Recommended wine: Johannisberg Riesling

4	whole manini (5 oz. ea.), cleaned and gutted
	Seasoned Flour (see Basic Recipes)
	salad oil for pan frying

Dredge manini in Seasoned Flour. Heat salad oil over medium heat and cook whole fish for 3-4 minutes on each side. Serve with Dried Shrimp Fern Shoot Salad. Serves 4-6

Dried Shrimp Fern Shoot Salad

1 bunch	fern shoots, cut into 1-in. pieces and blanched
1/4 cup	dried shrimp
1/2 cup	sliced red onions
1	vine-ripened tomato, cut into wedges
1/4 cup	soy sauce
1/4 cup	sugar
1 tbsp.	sesame oil
2 tbsp.	rice vinegar
	toasted sesame seeds (optional)

Combine ingredients and chill.

Recommended wine: Pinot Grigio

MAMA GUZMAN'S MANINI

In this light dish, the manini is braised, allowing the ginger and vinegar to permeate the fish.

6	whole manini (5 oz. ea.), gutted
3 tbsp.	salad oil
	salt and pepper to taste
1-1/2 cups	sliced yellow onions
1 tbsp.	minced ginger
6 tbsp.	white vinegar
5 cups	water

In a braising pot, heat the oil over medium heat. Season manini with salt and pepper and sear 1 minute on each side. Add onions, ginger and vinegar. Cover pot and let it steam for 3 minutes. Uncover then add water and simmer until 3/4 of it has evaporated. Serves 4-6.

Recommended wine: Johannisberg Riesling

THREADFIN

Moi

Because it's so versatile, threadfin, or moi, is one of my favorite fish to cook. I was introduced to this wonderful fish by my friend Ben Krause, owner of Pacific Harvest, a Big Island moi farm located in Kailua-Kona. Ben taught me all about moi and his special way of raising and nurturing them. Moi are primarily bottom feeders that use their threadlike pectoral rays as feelers, eating mostly shrimp, worms and small crabs. They are usually found in sandy areas close to shore. In ancient Hawai'i, moi were reserved for the ali'i, or chiefs. A commoner caught with a prized moi paid the consequences for violating this kapu. Today fish consumers can always find moi in Chinatown or can pre-order it from certain fish wholesalers. What I like about this fish is the way it holds up under any cooking method.

I've included a few simple recipes on the following pages. Moi gravlax is a great substitute for salmon and caviar. I've also added my Filipino-inspired moi ceviche, which is awesome for pūpū. Finally, a great way to celebrate Thanksgiving without turkey is to prepare a whole moi with rock shrimp stuffing.

FILIPINO-INFLUENCED MOI CEVICHE

The citrus juice of the calamansi is normally used as a condiment with the Filipino noodle dish known as pancit bihai. In this dish, it is used to lightly season the moi, as are the Chinese soy sauce and Thai sweet chili sauce.

16 oz.	moi sashimi
1/4 tsp.	thinly sliced shallots (may substitute yellow onions)
1/4 oz.	thinly sliced green onion
1 tbsp.	minced ginger
1/4 cup	calamansi juice
2 tbsp.	Chinese soy sauce
	sweet chili sauce to taste
	salt and black pepper to taste

Layer moi sashimi on a plate. Arrange shallots, green onion and ginger over moi. Pour calamansi juice over moi, then soy sauce. Dot each piece of fish with sweet chili sauce; sprinkle with salt and pepper. Let sit for 10-15 minutes before serving. Serves 4-6.

Recommended wine: Fumé Blanc

Gravlax is always a popular appetizer. This dish follows the traditional method of preparing gravlax but uses moi instead of salmon.

3-4	whole moi (16-20 oz. ea.), filleted with skin and scales on
	fresh cracked black pepper
	fresh minced dill
	(may substitute tarragon, thyme, chervil, etc.)
2 tbsp.	minced ginger
1/4 cup	truffle oil (optional)
4 tbsp.	sake or other liquor (optional)

Curing Mixture

1 cup	kosher salt
1 cup	granulated sugar

Place fillets on clear plastic wrap, skin side down. Sprinkle pepper over fish fillet. Rub dill and ginger into the fillet and splash with truffle oil and sake, if using. Combine kosher salt and sugar to make curing mixture. Cover each fillet completely with curing mixture (but don't cover the tail; it is so thin that it will be over-cured). Wrap fillets in plastic wrap and place on a flat surface for 6-7 hours in the refrigerator, until fish is translucent. Rinse curing salt off of fish with cold water. Cut fish into thin diagonal slices, but do not cut through the skin. Serve with toasted bagels, capers, onions and cream cheese. Serves 4-6.

Recommended wine: Fumé Blanc

For Thanksgiving or any occasion, surprise your diners with this moi dish, stuffed with a wealth of seafood. Garlic butter bastes the fish as it bakes.

4	whole moi (1-1/2 lbs. ea.), scaled and gutted
	salt and pepper
4 oz.	Rock Shrimp Stuffing
3/4 lb.	Basic Garlic Butter (see Basic Recipes)

Preheat oven to 325 degrees. Season cavity of moi with salt and pepper. Fill with stuffing. Season whole fish with more salt and pepper, then rub with Basic Garlic Butter. Place fish on a well-oiled baking pan. Bake for 20-25 minutes, until done. Serves 4-6.

Rock Shrimp Stuffing

1/4 cup	salad oil
1/2 cup	medium diced onion
1/2 cup	medium diced celery
1/2 cup	medium diced green bell pepper
5 oz.	rock shrimp
1 cup	chicken stock
1 tbsp.	Chef E Spice (see Basic Recipes)
3 cups	spiced croutons
1/2 tbsp.	minced garlic
1 tbsp.	salad oil
1/4 cup	Parmesan cheese
2 tbsp.	green onion
	splash of Worcestershire sauce
	splash of Tabasco sauce

Heat oil in a sauté pan. Sauté onions, celery and bell peppers for 2 minutes until translucent. Add rock shrimp and sauté for 3 minutes, then add chicken stock and Chef E Spice. Bring to a boil and fold in croutons. Stir in remaining ingredients, then remove from heat. Cool before stuffing fish. Use leftover stuffing as a side dish; or smother it with gravy, and it can be a meal by itself.

Recommended wine: Chardonnay

MOI SASHIMI WITH 3-CITRUS SAUCE

Sous chef Aaron Fukuda's sauce uses a trio of citruses to give this dish a well-balanced flavor.

16 oz.   moi sashimi

3-Citrus Sauce

3 tbsp.   apple cider vinegar
1/2 cup   salad oil
1/4 tsp.   chili flakes
                zest of 1 lime, 1 lemon and 1 orange
                juice of 1 lime, 1 lemon and 1 orange
                salt and fresh cracked black pepper to taste

Simple Syrup

                1/2 cup water
                1/2 cup sugar

To make Simple Syrup, bring water to a boil. Stir in sugar until dissolved. Cool. Combine syrup with all remaining sauce ingredients and mix well. Arrange moi sashimi on a bed of finely shredded cabbage. Pour 3-Citrus Sauce over fish. Serves 4-6.

Recommended wine: Johannisberg Riesling

WRASSE

'A'awa • Nabeta

Here I've included two types of wrasses: Hawaiian hogfish ('a'awa) and peacock wrasse (nabeta).

When we lived on the Big Island, my wife and I often enjoyed weekly fishing trips. We went regularly to Māhukona, a park on the Kohala Coast with cliffs of medium height and waters ten to 15 feet deep. As fishing rookies worried about getting our lines caught in the coral reefs, we found this to be an ideal fishing spot. There were always schools of papio, and we were usually lucky enough to catch Hawaiian hogfish, a great-tasting fish that comes in vibrant colors.

However, my favorite wrasse of all is the nabeta. I first heard about it through Paul Ah Cook, a good friend of mine. It is a high-priced, delicate fish. Paul got me hooked on preparing it in a way that makes its scales extra crispy and very enjoyable to eat.

MISOYAKI HOGFISH

The miso, sweetened with rice wine and vinegar, adds zest to the hogfish fillets.

6	hogfish fillets (3 oz. ea.)
4 oz.	Misoyaki Marinade

Misoyaki Marinade

2 tbsp.	mirin
1/4 cup	miso paste
2 tbsp.	rice wine vinegar
2 tbsp.	granulated sugar
1/8 tsp.	minced ginger

Combine marinade ingredients and mix well. Marinate fish for 1/2 hour. Place fish on a well-oiled sheet pan. Broil for 5-8 minutes. Serve with steamed rice. Serves 4-6.

Recommended wine: Chardonnay

ISLAND-STYLE HOGFISH PO' BOY

The Po' Boy is a Louisiana-style sandwich traditionally made with pork. This recipe substitutes hogfish to create an equally hearty sandwich.

6	hogfish fillets (3 oz. ea., from 3 8- to 10-oz. whole fish)
1 cup	buttermilk
	salt and pepper to taste
2 cups	cornmeal
1 cup	salad oil
6-8 in.	toasted french bread
6	tomato slices
6	lettuce leaves
1 cup	Namasu Tartar

Soak fillets in buttermilk seasoned with salt and pepper for 1 hour. Drain hogfish and dredge in cornmeal. Shake off excess. In a pan, heat oil to 325 degrees, until the oil sizzles when sprinkled with cornmeal. Pan-fry fish for 2-3 minutes on each side. Drain on paper towels and season with more salt and pepper. Serve fillets on French bread with tomato, lettuce and Namasu Tartar sauce. Serves 4-6.

Namasu Tartar

8 oz.	prepared cucumber namasu, drained (found at Asian grocery stores)
2 cups	mayonnaise
2 tbsp.	capers
	juice of 1/2 lemon
1/3 cup	namasu liquid (optional)

With a knife, rough chop namasu and combine with remaining ingredients. Use namasu liquid to thin the tartar sauce. (Note: Leftover Namasu Tartar sauce is a great substitute for traditional tartar sauce, delicious with baked fish fillets or deep-fried whole fish.)

Recommended wine: Chardonnay

BEER-BATTERED HAWAIIAN HOGFISH WITH KALAMATA OLIVE SAUCE

This one makes a great entree or appetizer for a Super Bowl party or any other informal get-together.

6   hogfish fillets (3 oz. ea., from 3 8- to 10-oz. whole fish)
            oil for frying
            Seasoned Flour (see Basic Recipes)

Beer Batter

3 cups   beer
2 cups   flour
1   egg
1/4 cup   salad oil
            pinch of salt

Preheat oil to 325 to 350 degrees. To make batter, combine all ingredients and mix well. Dredge hogfish in seasoned flour and shake off excess. Dip into Beer Batter and deep-fry for 4-6 minutes until golden brown. Serve with Kalamata Olive Sauce. Serves 4-6.

Kalamata Olive Sauce

2 cups   mayonnaise
1 tbsp.   ketchup
1 tbsp.   whole grain mustard
2 tbsp.   minced celery
2 tbsp.   minced onions
2 tsp.   minced basil
1/2 tsp.   minced garlic
2 tbsp.   minced kalamata olives
            juice of 1/2 lemon
1 tbsp.   minced green bell pepper (optional)

Combine all ingredients.

Recommended wine: Fumé Blanc

6	hogfish fillets (3 oz., from 3 8- to 10-oz. whole fish)
	Dijon mustard
	salt and pepper to taste
3	Idaho potatoes, peeled and curled
	(use Japanese mandoline)
3 oz.	salad oil

Season fillets with salt and pepper. Brush both sides with mustard. Wrap fillets in potato strings to cover completely. Heat oil over medium heat and pan-fry fillets for 3-4 minutes per side, until golden brown. Serve with Bacon-Chive Sour Cream Sauce. Serves 4-6. (Note: If you don't have a mandoline, use the coarse side of a box grater.)

Bacon-Chive Sour Cream Sauce

1 cup	sour cream
1/4 cup	sliced chives
1/2 cup	apple wood-smoked bacon, cooked and minced
1/4 cup	Basic Fish Stock (see Basic Recipes; may
	substitute water)
	salt and fresh cracked black pepper to taste

Combine all ingredients and serve at room temperature.

Recommended wine: Fumé Blanc

PAN-FRIED WHOLE NABETA WITH SIMPLE CHILI-SOY SAUCE

3-4	whole nabeta, gutted with scales left on
	salt and pepper to taste
	Seasoned Flour (see Basic Recipes)
	salad oil for pan-frying

Simple Chili Soy Sauce

1 cup	soy sauce
2	sliced Hawaiian chili peppers
	juice of 1/2 lime
1 tbsp.	sliced green onion
	pinch sugar

Season fish with salt and pepper. Dredge in Seasoned Flour; shake off excess. Heat oil in sauté pan. Pan-fry fish for 3-4 minutes on each side, until golden brown (with scales left on, proper cooking will result in a crispy texture). Combine sauce ingredients and pour over fish. Serves 4-6.

Recommended wine: Fumé Blanc

Nabeta has soft scales. Leave them on, then fry the fish and you'll find the dish has a nice crunch.

4-6	nabeta fillets (4 oz., from 3-4 1-lb. fish), skin and scales left on
2 tbsp.	salad oil
	salt and pepper to taste
2-1/2 cups	blanched Chinese snow peas, chilled

In a sauté pan, heat oil over medium-high heat. Sear nabeta, skin side down, until edges are golden. Turn and sear another 2-3 minutes. Season with salt and pepper on skin side. Place fish on snow peas and drizzle with Tahini Miso Dressing. Serves 4-6.

Tahini Miso Dressing

1/2 cup	mayonnaise
1 tbsp.	miso
3/4 cup	tahini (sesame paste)
1/4 cup	water
1 tbsp.	rice vinegar
1/8 cup	sugar
1 tbsp.	toasted sesame seeds
	salt and pepper to taste

Combine all ingredients and mix well.

Recommended wine: Fumé Blanc

Basic Recipes

ASIAN OIL

1/2 cup	minced ginger
1/2 cup	minced green onion
2 tbsp.	sesame oil
1/2 cup	minced cilantro
1/2 cup	salad oil
	salt and pepper to taste

In a bowl, combine ginger, green onion, sesame oil and cilantro. Heat salad oil in a saucepan until smoking. Slowly pour hot oil into ginger mixture, stirring as you pour. Season with salt and pepper.

BASIC BUTTER SAUCE

Prepare this sauce 1 hour in advance. It may be kept warm in a thermos.

1/4 cup	minced shallot (may substitute minced onion)
1/2 cup	white wine
1/4 tsp.	minced garlic
1 sprig	thyme
1	bay leaf
3	black peppercorns
	juice of 1 lemon
1/3 cup	heavy cream
1/2 block	butter (cold, diced)
	salt and pepper to taste

In a non-reactive pot, combine all ingredients except cream, butter, salt and pepper, and reduce until liquid is almost evaporated. Add cream and reduce by half. Reduce heat to low and slowly whisk in butter until incorporated. Season with salt and pepper; strain.

BASIC FISH STOCK

2 tbsp.	salad oil
1/2 cup	onions, chopped fine
1/4 cup	celery, chopped fine
1/4 cup	leeks, chopped fine
4-6 lbs.	fish bones
	carrot and mushroom trimmings (optional)
1/2 cup	white wine
1 gallon	water
1	small bay leaf
1/4 tsp.	whole black peppercorns
2 sprigs	thyme

In a stock pot, place oil, onions, celery, leeks, fish bones, and carrot and mushroom trimmings, if using. Set pot on low heat and cook slowly for 5 minutes, until bones are opaque. Add wine and bring to a simmer. Add water to cover the ingredients and add spices. Simmer for 30-45 minutes. Strain and cool broth over an ice bath. (Note: Do not bring the stock to a boil at any point or it will become cloudy.)

BASIC GARLIC BUTTER

2-1/2 lb.	unsalted butter, at room temperature
1/4 cup	minced garlic
2 tbsp.	minced parsley
2 tsp.	salt
1 tsp.	ground black pepper
1 tbsp.	Worcestershire sauce
2 tsp.	Tabasco sauce

Combine all ingredients and mix well.

BASIC HAWAIIAN CHILI PEPPER REMOULADE

Remoulade is a condiment served with Louisiana's famous boiled shrimp. This creamy, piquant sauce comes in many variations, depending on the region. I've added Hawaiian chili pepper water for an Island flavor.

1/2 cup	minced celery
1/2 cup	minced green bell peppers
1/2 cup	minced onions
1 tsp.	minced garlic
1 cup	green onions
3 cups	mayonnaise
1 cup	ketchup
4 tbsp.	whole-grain mustard
3 tbsp.	Hawaiian chili pepper water
1-1/2 tbsp.	Worcestershire sauce
1-1/2 tsp.	Tabasco sauce
1/2 tsp.	salt
	juice of 1/2 lemon

Combine all ingredients and mix well.

BASIC HERB OIL

4 cups	salad oil or virgin olive oil or garlic oil
3 sprigs	fresh rosemary
2 cloves	garlic, slightly crushed
5 sprigs	thyme
5	black peppercorns

Combine ingredients and refrigerate.

BASIC OVEN-ROASTED VEGETABLE SALAD

3	medium zucchini, quartered (pieces should be 3 in. long)
3	medium yellow squash, quartered (pieces should be 3 in. long)
1	medium red onion, cut in 1/2-in. slices
2 cups	button mushrooms
1/4 cup	garlic cloves
2 tbsp.	Basic Herb Oil (see Basic Recipes)
1 tbsp.	Chef E Spice (see Basic Recipes)
2 tbsp.	sliced garlic chives
1 tbsp.	balsamic vinegar
	salt and pepper to taste

Preheat oven to 350 degrees. Place all vegetables and garlic in a bowl and lightly coat with herb oil. Season with Chef E Spice. Place vegetables on a sheet pan and cook for 20-30 minutes, stirring every 10 minutes. Return vegetables to a bowl. Sprinkle with garlic chives and balsamic vinegar. Season with salt and pepper. Serve at room temperature. Serves 4-6.

BASIC TERIYAKI SAUCE

1 cup	soy sauce
1 cup	sugar
2 cups	water
	juice from whole lemon
1 finger	ginger, smashed
4 cloves	garlic, smashed
1/4 cup	cornstarch dissolved in 1/4 cup water

Combine all ingredients except cornstarch slurry; let sit 24 hours. Strain sauce. Bring to a boil in a saucepan and thicken gradually with cornstarch mixture to desired consistency.

CHEF E SPICE

6-1/2 cups	iodized salt
3-1/4 cups	paprika
1/2 cup	cayenne
2-1/2 cups	ground black pepper
2-1/2 cups	granulated garlic
1-1/2 cups	onion powder
4 cups	dried oregano
4 cups	dried thyme
3/4 cup	togarashi (Japanese seasoning)

Combine all ingredients.

FRIED GARLIC

1 cup	minced garlic
4 cups	salad oil

In a wok, combine garlic and oil. Bring the temperature to high and whisk for 6 minutes, or until the garlic is golden brown. Strain. Place fried garlic on a dry towel and pat dry. Crumble garlic to separate. Reserve oil for Basic Herb Oil (see Basic Recipes).

SEASONED FLOUR

2 cups	flour
1 cup	cornstarch
1 tbsp.	Chef E Spice (see Basic Recipes)
1/2 tbsp.	salt

Combine all ingredients.

SHELLFISH STOCK

1/2 cup	salad oil
1 gallon	packed shrimp shells (may substitute lobster or blue crab shells)
4 cups	diced yellow onions
3 cups	diced celery
4 cups	diced fennel bulb (optional)
2	bay leaves
1 tbsp.	black peppercorn
1/3 cup	minced garlic, packed
1 cup	tomato paste
3 cups	Pernod liqueur (may substitute white wine)
1-1/2 gallon	water
1 cup	packed fresh thyme or dried thyme sprigs

In a stock pot, heat salad oil until smoking. Add shrimp shells and sauté for 5 minutes. Add onions, celery, fennel (if using), bay leaves and peppercorns. Sauté for 5 minutes. Add garlic and cook for 2 minutes. Add tomato paste and cook for 3 minutes. Deglaze pot with Pernod and cook until liquid is almost evaporated. Add water and thyme; simmer for 20 minutes. Strain.

TEMPURA BATTER

1	egg
1 cup	cold water
1/2 cup	flour
1/2 cup	corn starch
1 tsp.	salt

Beat egg and water. Add to dry ingredients and mix well. Chill batter for at least 1 hour before using.

aioli	garlic mayonnaise originating in Provence in southern France
balsamic vinegar	Trebbiano grape vinegar aged in barrels of varying size and kinds of wood; pungent and dark in color
basil	member of the mint family with a pungent flavor described as a cross between licorice and cloves
beurre blanc	"white butter," a classic French reduction of wine, vinegar and shallots; white chunks of cold butter whisked until thick and smooth, with heavy cream often added to stabilize sauce
bok choy	Chinese cabbage
bouillabaisse	a celebrated seafood stew originating in Provence, an assortment of fish, shellfish, onions, tomatoes, white wine, olive oil, garlic, saffron and herbs; traditionally ladled over thick slices of French bread
chiso	aromatic green, jagged-edged leaf of the perilla (beefsteak) plant related to mint and basil; often served with sushi
choi sum	Chinese broccoli, similar to bok choy
fennel	aromatic plant with pale green celery-like stems, bright green feathery foliage, and a sweeter and more delicate flavor than anise; sometimes referred to as "sweet anise"

fish sauce	condiment or flavoring made from various mixtures of liquids from salted, fermented fish; popular throughout Southeast Asia
furikake	Japanese blend of dried seasonings including tuna flakes, ground sesame seeds, crumbled seaweed and salt
Hawaiian chili pepper	small, spicy, red-orange pepper used as a lively seasoning
kaffir lime	small, pear-shaped citrus fruit — bright yellow-green, bumpy and wrinkled — grown in Southeast Asia and Hawai'i; glossy green leaves used in cooking give off intense, floral-lemon fragrance
kālua pig	Hawaiian whole roasted pig, traditionally slow-baked in an earthen pit oven, covered with hot coals or kiawe wood and banana or ti leaves
katsu	breaded in Japanese panko crumbs and crispy fried
kiawe	fragrant grilling wood from the mesquite (algaroba) tree, which grows abundantly in Hawai'i
konbu	dried seaweed
kosher salt	pure refined rock salt used for pickling because it contains no magnesium carbonate and thus does not cloud brine solutions
limu	branch-like seaweed found in Hawaiian waters

lumpia	wrappers for Filipino egg rolls or spring rolls, about 8 inches square; made of flour or corn-starch, eggs and water
mirepoix	mixture of diced carrots, onions, celery and herbs sauteed in butter, sometimes including ham or bacon; used to season sauces, soups and stews and as a bed on which to braise meats or fish
miso	thick paste of salted and fermented soybeans and rice or barley; includes white miso — sweet and fine-textured and used for soups, dressings and grilled foods — and the saltier red miso, also good in soups
nage	flavored broth
nori	dried, thin sheets of black-green seaweed, frequently used in Japanese cooking, often for wrapping sushi; used as seasoning or a garnish when finely cut
ogo	seaweed (Japanese)
panko	crispy, Japanese-style bread crumbs
poke	cubed raw fish made with onions and seaweed, usually served as an appetizer or in salads
Portuguese sausage	pork sausage heavily spiced with red pepper
ragout	thick, rich, well-seasoned stew, usually containing meat, poultry or fish; made with or without vegetables

remoulade	classic French sauce combining mayonnaise (usually homemade), mustard, capers, chopped gherkins, herbs and anchovies; served chilled with cold meats, fish or shellfish
saffron	yellow-orange stigmas from a small, purple crocus; the world's most expensive spice, used primarily to flavor and tint food
sashimi	thinly sliced raw fish
shichimi	mixture of sansho (mildly hot Japanese seasoning from the berries of the prickly ash tree), orange peel, poppy seeds, white and black sesame seeds, chili pepper and seaweed; Japanese for "seven spices" or "seven flavors"
shiitake	dark brown mushroom with a full-bodied, bosky flavor, originating in Japan and Korea, averaging 3 to 6 inches in diameter
star anise	licorice-flavored, distinctively shaped pod with eight points
truffle	fungus with an earthy, garlicky aroma and flavor; grows 3 to 12 inches underground, near the roots of trees, and is rooted out by specially trained dogs and pigs; nearly 70 known varieties worldwide
wakame	thin seaweed used primarily in soups and salads
wasabi	Japanese horseradish made from the root of an Asian plant sometimes shredded as a garnish

INDEX

As a boy growing up in Kahului, Maui, Elmer Guzman had a passion for Hawai'i's reef and shoreline fish and for fresh island produce. Today, his innovative Hawaiian Regional Cuisine at Sam Choy's Diamond Head Restaurant — where he serves as executive chef — is a natural extension of this boyhood passion. His reef fish tastings and nightly specials are popular features at the acclaimed Honolulu restaurant.

A graduate of the Kapi'olani Community College Culinary Arts program, Elmer worked in the early 1990s under renowned chef Alan Wong, at the Mauna Lani Bay Resort & Bungalows on the Big Island of Hawai'i. He apprenticed at the prestigious Greenbriar Hotel at White Sulphur Springs, West Virginia, where he graduated with high honors, then served as sous chef at Emeril's Restaurant in New Orleans, Louisiana, where he worked under television personality and award-winning chef Emeril Lagasse.

When Chef Elmer isn't creating new dishes in the kitchen, he enjoys fishing on the reef with his wife, Samantha, and their young daughters, Tatiana and Tatum.

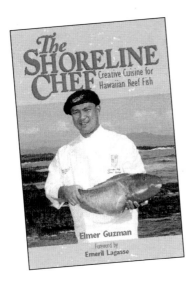

SHARE
THE SHORELINE CHEF
WITH FAMILY
AND FRIENDS!